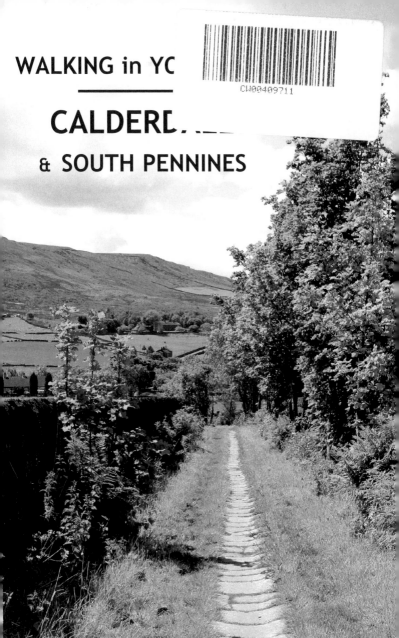

WALKING in YC

CALDERD...

& SOUTH PENNINES

HILLSIDE GUIDES - ACROSS THE NORTH

Yorkshire River Photobooks
•JOURNEY OF THE WHARFE

Easy Walks •50 YORKSHIRE WALKS FOR ALL

Walking in Yorkshire - North/East (25 Walks)
•NORTH YORK MOORS South/West   •NORTH YORK MOORS North/East
•YORKSHIRE WOLDS   •HOWARDIAN HILLS & VALE OF YORK

Walking in Yorkshire - West/South/Mid (25 Walks)
•AIRE VALLEY & BRONTE COUNTRY   •HARROGATE & ILKLEY
•CALDERDALE & SOUTH PENNINES   •SOUTH YORKSHIRE

Walking in Yorkshire - Yorkshire Dales (25 Walks)
•East: NIDDERDALE & RIPON   •West: THREE PEAKS & HOWGILL FELLS
•South: WHARFEDALE & MALHAM •North: WENSLEYDALE & SWALEDALE

Circular Walks - Lancashire/North West/North Pennines
•BOWLAND   •PENDLE & RIBBLE   •ARNSIDE & SILVERDALE
•LUNESDALE   •EDEN VALLEY   •ALSTON & ALLENDALE

Long Distance Walks
•COAST TO COAST WALK •DALES WAY •CUMBRIA WAY
•PENDLE WAY   •CALDERDALE WAY

Hillwalking - Lake District (25 Walks)
•LAKELAND FELLS - SOUTH   •LAKELAND FELLS - EAST
•LAKELAND FELLS - NORTH   •LAKELAND FELLS - WEST

Short Scenic Walks (30 Walks)
•NORTH YORK MOORS   •HARROGATE & NIDDERDALE

Short Scenic Walks (20 Walks)
•UPPER WHARFEDALE •INGLETON/WESTERN DALES •RIBBLESDALE
•MALHAMDALE   •SWALEDALE   •SEDBERGH/DENTDALE
•UPPER WENSLEYDALE •LOWER WENSLEYDALE
•ILKLEY/WASHBURN VALLEY •AIRE VALLEY •HAWORTH
•HEBDEN BRIDGE •AROUND PENDLE •RIBBLE VALLEY •BOWLAND

*Send for a detailed current catalogue and price list
and also visit www.hillsidepublications.co.uk*

WALKING in YORKSHIRE

CALDERDALE
& SOUTH PENNINES

Paul Hannon

Hillside

HILLSIDE PUBLICATIONS

2 New School Lane
Cullingworth
Bradford
West Yorkshire
BD13 5DA

First published 2019

© Paul Hannon 2019   ISBN 978-1-907626-20-3

Cover illustrations: Upper Calderdale; Colne Valley near Slaithwaite
Back cover: Castle Hill; Page One: Langfield Common from Mankinholes
Page Three: Stoodley Pike; Above: Hebble Hole Bridge; Opposite: Lumbutts
(Paul Hannon/Yorkshire Photo Library)

The sketch maps are based on 1947 Ordnance Survey One-Inch maps

Printed in China on behalf of Latitude Press

CONTENTS

INTRODUCTION

The South Pennines is a vast area sandwiched between the Yorkshire Dales and the Peak District National Parks. Such is the northerly march of the latter that four of these walks reach within its bounds, though there is an undeniable 'Pennine' rather than 'Peak' feel to the surrounds. The area explored within these pages constitutes the southern bulk of the South Pennines, based around the Calder, Colne and Holme Valleys. Between here and the Dales, Yorkshire's remaining South Pennines feature in the companion volume *Aire Valley & Bronte Country*.

The heart of this region is Calderdale, focused on Hebden Bridge and Todmorden, with the Calder slowly leaving the hill country for the towns of Sowerby Bridge, Halifax, Brighouse and Elland. The Holme Valley is based on Holmfirth, and the Colne Valley on Marsden, the two merging in Huddersfield before joining the Calder. Just some of the highlights of this fascinating region are the landmark towers found on Stoodley Pike and Castle Hill, the National Trust's colourful Marsden Moor, the wonders of Standedge Tunnel, the rich woodland of Hardcastle Crags, and absorbing villages such as Ripponden, Heptonstall, Luddenden, Upperthong and Holme.

The area oozes character, borne in no small way out of the Industrial Revolution. Even seemingly far from the larger mill-towns that were at the heart of that sweeping change, one is never far from its evidence, be it canals, reservoirs, quarries, turnpike roads or packhorse trails, as well as hamlets where handloom weaving thrived in beautiful three-storeyed houses of which many survive. The hillsides are laced with a network of centuries-old trade routes used mainly by packhorses: many stone causeways have survived, laying dormant in wait for today's foot-traveller. Hugging the valley bottoms, in contrast, are the Rochdale and Huddersfield Canals, which largely replaced packhorse routes and whose colourful towpaths now provide miles of leisurely walking.

Tumbling to the floor of the upper dales are short-lived but deep-cut and richly wooded little valleys known as cloughs, where early water-powered mills were built in the most unlikely settings. Up on the tops one is never far from a reservoir, the earlier ones made to serve the canals, others to slake the ever-growing thirsts of expanding towns and their textile mills. This is solid gritstone

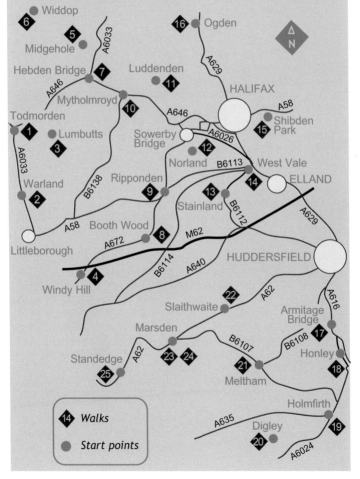

WALKING in YORKSHIRE

CALDERDALE & SOUTH PENNINES

N

Widdop
6
5
Midgehole
Hebden Bridge 7
Luddenden
16 Ogden
11
HALIFAX
A6033
A646
Mytholmroyd 10
A646
A58
Todmorden
1
Lumbutts
Sowerby Bridge
A6026
Shibden Park
15
3
12
Norland
B6113
West Vale
Warland
Ripponden
9
14
ELLAND
2
13
Stainland
B6112
A629
B6138
Booth Wood
8
M62
A58
A672
B6114
A640
HUDDERSFIELD
Littleborough
Windy Hill 4
Slaithwaite
22
A62
Armitage Bridge
A616
Marsden
B6107
B6108
17
Honley
Standedge
A62
23 24
21
18
25
Meltham
Holmfirth
A635
Digley
19
20
A6024

Walks 14

Start points

7

country, and sharing the higher ground with the reservoirs are many clusters of boulders and crags, with the weathered natural outcrops such as the Bride Stones, Buckstones and Blackstone Edge outshining the countless sites of former quarries that provided the material for the drystone walls, reservoirs and buildings.

Principal river of the region, the Calder absorbs countless side valleys carved out by the likes of Walsden Water, Hebden Water, Cragg Brook, Luddenden Brook and Shibden Brook. In the Calder Valley in particular, larger settlements squeeze into the cramped valley floor, shared with river, canal, road and railway. Steep flanks rise to intervening ledges where older villages, predecessors of their bigger brothers below, almost shake hands across the deep divides. Higher still, rough pasture gives way to open moorland, where the mill chimney 2 miles away might as well be 200 miles distant. The South Pennines' fascination is its unique blend of town and country: the two are inextricably linked, and one can revel in a feast of fascinating walking.

Access to the countryside

The majority of walks are on public rights of way with no access restrictions, or long-established access areas and paths. A handful also take advantage of Right to Roam: any walks making use of Open Country are noted as such in their introduction, though on most days of the year you are free to walk responsibly over these wonderfully invigorating landscapes. Of the restrictions that do pertain, the two most notable are that dogs are normally banned from grouse moors (other than on rights of way); and that the areas can be closed to walkers for up to 28 days each year, subject to advance notice. The most likely times will be from the 'Glorious Twelfth', the start of the grouse shooting season in August, though weekends should largely be unaffected. Further information can be obtained from Natural England, and ideally from information centres. Finally, bear in mind that in spring, avoiding tramping over open country away from paths helps safeguard the vulnerable ground-nesting birds.

Bus services within the area are generally good, and availability is mentioned in the introduction to each walk, where relevant. Thanks to the proximity of some large centres of population, many railway stations are also useful.

Using the guide

The walks range from 5½ to 7¼ miles, the average distance being around 6 miles. Each walk is self-contained, with essential information being followed by a concise route description and a simple map. Dovetailed in between are snippets of information on features along the way: these are placed in *italics* to ensure that the all important route description is easier to locate. Start point postcodes are a rough guide only for those with 'satnav': grid references are more precise! The sketch maps serve to identify the location of the routes rather than the fine detail, and whilst the description should be sufficient to guide you around, an Ordnance Survey map is recommended. To gain the most from a walk, the detail of a 1:25,000 scale Explorer map is unsurpassed. It also gives the option to vary walks as desired, giving a much improved picture of your surroundings and the availability of any linking paths for shortening or lengthening walks. Three maps cover all the walks:

- *Explorer OL1 - Peak District, Dark Peak*
- *Explorer OL21 - South Pennines (17 of the 25 walks)*
- *Explorer 288 - Bradford & Huddersfield*

Also useful for planning are Landranger maps 103, 104 and 110.

Useful contacts

Information Centres

Visitor & Canal Centre **Hebden Bridge** HX7 8AF • 01422-843831
15 Burnley Road **Todmorden** OL14 7BU • 01706-818181
Central Library, Square Road **Halifax** HX1 1QG • 01422-368725
Library, Mechanics Hall, Peel Street **Marsden** HD7 6BW • 01484-222555
Library, 47 Huddersfield Road **Holmfirth** HD9 3JH • 01484-223200
Library, Princess Alexandra Walk **Huddersfield** HD1 2SU • 01484-223200
Open Access • 0845-100 3298   www.countrysideaccess.gov.uk

WALK 1

BRIDE STONES

A fine ramble around old hillside packways and outcrops

START *Todmorden (SD 936241; OL14 5AA)*

DISTANCE *6^{1}4 miles (10km)*

ORDNANCE SURVEY 1:25,000 MAP
Explorer OL21 - South Pennines

ACCESS *Start from the town centre. Car parks. Bus and train from Halifax, Rochdale and Burnley. • OPEN ACCESS: see page 8.*

The little town of Todmorden is based around its Town Hall of 1875, with marble figures on a pediment above tall columns. The Old Hall of 1603 has an intricate frontage of gables and mullioned and transomed windows. St Mary's church is central but eclipsed by the tall-spired Unitarian Church of 1869. Unlike its counterparts that thrived on the woollen industry, Todmorden's mills were geared to Lancashire's cotton industry: indeed until the late 19th century it was literally on the border. Of the three roads heading out, two aim for the red rose towns of Rochdale and Burnley, both more accessible than Todmorden's Yorkshire masters in Halifax: a hint of divided loyalties still remains! Todmorden was the birthplace of Incredible Edible, a community project campaigning for local food. From small beginnings in 2008, people began growing produce in nooks and crannies, making valuable use of tiny pockets of spare land. The project has now mushroomed around the globe.

From the Town Hall roundabout head north on the Burnley road, passing beneath the rail viaduct by the bus station. Just after, turn right on Stansfield Road, bridging the River Calder. At the end it swings left to a junction. Go right a short way to the road-end at the railway line, and use a tall footbridge to cross it. On the other side advance to suburban Stansfield Hall Road. Go briefly right and then take an access road on the left, leaving at once for a steep flight of stone steps climbing up onto an access road. Go right up past the houses of The Mount, and when this ends a path takes over into trees. This runs a level, enclosed course to very quickly reach a cross-paths. Turn left for the next stage of the climb, largely enclosed and in its upper section alongside a heather bank, emerging onto a level way at the top alongside Todmorden golf course.

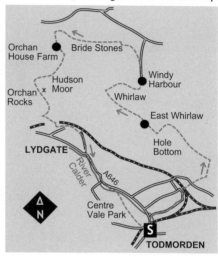

Go left beneath more heather, quickly emerging at the top of a heathery bank. Take either path in front, along the bank top or the enclosed way, as they soon merge again at the end beneath scattered rocks. Advance on, the way becoming more enclosed and broader as it rises then drops gently to an access road climbing to the solitary house on the right at Wickenberry Clough. Cross straight over, the access road rising above a wood to approach East Whirlaw Farm. Just past it as the rough road swings sharp right for Cally Hall Farm, go left on a briefly enclosed path to a bridle-gate/stile. Now as Whirlaw Lane, the path continues either side of a wall above East Whirlaw. Ignoring a rough track climbing right, it runs to a bridle-gate onto the heathery slopes of Whirlaw Common. *This section of the Pennines is criss-crossed by a network of old*

packhorse routes by which traders would lead horses laden with all manner of goods from town to town and farm to farm. Like many others this features a well-preserved stone causeway – or causey – on which the pack ponies would be able to find firm footing over less solid terrain.

The path rises away as a superb flagged trod curving up the moor beneath Whirlaw Stones to reach a gate at the far end. Ignore this and double back right up the moor, an early flagged section then rising past boulders on the right and joined by a fence. Up to your left are the Bride Stones. Levelling out, the grassy path runs on the fenceside to a gate onto the head of a farm track. Follow this along to quickly reach a surfaced road end at a carved stone gatepost. Ignore the inviting grassy continuation, and turn left up the punishingly steep road past Windy Harbour Farm. On easing out at Mast Farm continue on, but at the gentle brow make use of Open Access and take a stile on the left – the Bride Stones await just ahead. A thin trod bears gently right to a stile at a fence/wall corner, then resumes running left with the fence on Bride Stones Moor. Level with the first boulders just above, leave the little path and rise the short way to the first ones.

The Great Bride Stones are an extensive group of rocks, and the first of these include a remarkable detached rock resembling its North York Moors' namesakes. Advance on along the crest to the Ordnance Survey column at 1437ft/438m marking the high point of the walk. Resume along the crest, with the main path set a little back from the edge. The path declines gently with further lower outcrops below, and heads on through two very faint old walls. You soon arrive at a further cluster in line with Coal Clough windfarm immediately above two houses on a plantation edge at Orchan House Farm. *An unofficial short-cut uses a grassy path down the bank from these rocks to meet the access road below.*

A broader green path resumes, dropping slightly to a gate off the moor. Joining an access track on the edge of the wood, drop left down this to Orchan House Farm, passing between the houses and out into a field below those final rocks. Here leave it in favour of a grass track dropping right, down the field centre to a gate/stile and down a rougher pasture to a gateway onto Stony Lane. This continuation of the way you left at Whirlaw is met at a crossroads of ways, with Orchan Rocks visible below. Take none, instead pass through a bridle-gate/stile in front on a path bearing right across heathery Hudson Moor. Occasionally moist, it quickly drops to the moor edge at stone-arched Hudson Bridge, a grand spot for a break. Don't cross, but take the clear path doubling back left. This runs a super course slanting steadily down through the heather. *Orchan Rocks are just visible to the left.* Reaching a wall at the bottom, go left a few strides to a gate in it. A splendid fenceside grass track now drops down below a further heathery bank, meeting a broad path coming down from the left. Passing through a gate/stile at the bottom corner you join an access road from the left.

Turn down this enclosed course of Jumps Lane, very quickly absorbing Jumps Farm's drive and leading all the way down to the valley, largely through the trees of Kitson Wood. *During this stage there is a good view of the railway viaduct, while the railway itself later passes through a deep tunnel directly beneath you.* As civilisation is embraced turn left after the first house on the access road of Church Hill, dropping down onto the end of Church Road. Go straight ahead here for a few yards on a private-looking drive at Owlers Walk. An enclosed path passes right of the last house and on beneath a rail embankment to emerge alongside an immense railway arch. Turn right on Stoney Royd Lane, quickly absorbing a driveway and leading out through suburbia to the main road at Lydgate.

Cross and go left for a few minutes, on a wide verge path by the River Calder. Past a school and then Ewood Lane, enter Central Vale Park at North Lodge. *Bought from the Fielden family in 1910, the park features a statue of John Fielden, MP for Oldham: he was instrumental in the passing of the 10 Hour Act in 1847, which meant women and children were saved from working more than 10 hours per day!* You can find your own way from here, emerging at the end to continue the final few minutes back into the centre of town. Best option is to aim for the church tower, leaving the right-hand corner of the park behind a skateboard area. Rising briefly to a level path, this goes left into trees behind the cricket club to emerge on the end of Well Lane above the redundant Christ Church of 1834. Keep straight on, and towards the end drop left down the steep Ridge Steps onto Ridge Road. Go left under the rail bridge to pass the White Hart pub and emerge opposite the town hall.

WALSDEN MOOR

From towpath to moor top, and a historic packhorse trail

START *Warland (SD 944201; OL14 6UP)*

DISTANCE *5³⁄4 miles (9¹⁄4km)*

ORDNANCE SURVEY 1:25,000 MAP
Explorer OL21 - South Pennines

ACCESS *Start from the former Bird i'th' Hand pub on A6033. Parking verge south of ex-pub opposite road-end, outside of yellow lines: lay-by a little to north. Todmorden-Rochdale bus.*

From the former pub cross the road and take the lane (Warland Gate End) heading away to cross the Rochdale Canal alongside Warland Upper Lock. *The bridge marks the county boundary, also confirmed by a modern boundary stone. Completed in 1804, the canal runs 33 miles between Manchester and Sowerby Bridge. Its heyday was a brief one, and the demise began in 1841 when the Lancashire & Yorkshire Railway arrived, and by 1922 commercial traffic had virtually ceased. Today it is a colourful leisure facility with a succession of narrow locks bringing it down from its summit a little further south at Littleborough.*

Keep on the lane between two houses as it starts a long climb to the moor, with an early view down to the canal. *Whitewashed cottages on the left at a sharp bend feature a 1655 datestone.* At a very brief levelling out take the right-hand gate at a fork, bridging a stream to rise again to a sharp bend right towards Calflee House. Don't follow the drive to it, but take a gate on the left and follow the right-hand track rising to a gate in the wall above. Through this turn sharp right on a grassy way, passing through another gate to a restored house above Calflee House. Pass to its rear to a gate/stile above its rear corner, and after a few reeds a path slants up the grassy moor with a fence to a gate above. The path now rises with a wall then fence on your left, in harmony with the adjacent stream.

The going quickly eases and Warland Reservoir's retaining wall is equally quickly revealed ahead. On nearing the embankment, rise gently right on a broad track to gain the reservoir's southern corner. *Far to the north Coal Clough windfarm spreads itself across the noble breast of Pendle Hill, with Scout Moor windfarm to the west.* Cross straight over the reservoir road and over a connecting footbridge onto a thin path along the grassy embankment of Light Hazzles Reservoir on your right. *Both reservoirs were built in 1804 to supply the canal.*

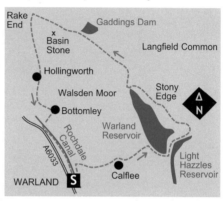

At the far end of the reedy reservoir head, the path advances the short way to a wooden footbridge over a small clough. The clear path bears off to the left on the distinct embankment of a long-defunct drain. It runs a dead-level course into increasing heather. Nearing Warland Reservoir again you pass just below extensive boulder-slopes at Stony Edge. *Here you find heather and gritstone in harmony, a good place for a break.* The reservoir track is regained upon bridging a concrete drain at the most northerly point of the reservoir. Follow the hard track right just as far as a sharp bend. *Stoodley Pike appears almost at once, some way ahead along the moorland of Langfield Common.* Here strike left across the moor on a firmly flagged path descending very gently in the direction of Gaddings Dam. The flags lead unfailingly down until you leave peaty, moist moor for flat, dry grassy moor, and a good path runs on to traverse the left-hand embankment.

Below a grandiose flight of steps the broader path continues down the moor towards the distinctive Basin Stone: a brief fork left reaches it. The main path trends right down to a path crossroads marked by a cairn at Rake End. *From here towards Bottomley you follow the well-preserved causeway of Salter Rake Gate, part of a packhorse route used largely for bringing salt across the Pennines from Cheshire: it has a bird's-eye view of Walsden and across the valley to Ramsden Clough.* Turn left on the path sloping down the moor, a grand stride acquiring a continuous stone-flagged surface before entering walled confines at North Hollingworth. Advance a short way along the first drive, and at the junction, with a white-walled, mullioned windowed old house in front, go left on the drive to the road-end at isolated Hollingworth Gate.

From a gate beneath the house ignore the wide track up the field, and instead trace the re-emergent causeway along the field bottom to a bridle-gate at the end. *This is an excellent viewpoint, with the canal leading the eye through the Walsden Gorge, and the buttress of Reddyshore Scout opposite.* The causey descends to the house at Dean Royd, where contour along the rear before rising left to a brow. The path then curves around to a small bridge in Bottomley Clough, across which it rises into the hamlet of Bottomley. Turn right just a few strides then leave the access road by a gate on the right. An enclosed, setted way descends to the canal at Bottomley Lock. *Hidden in a field is the entrance to Summit railway tunnel, scene of a dramatic train fire in 1984.* Cross the bridge and go left on the towpath to return to Warland, passing Warland Lower Lock and a reedy pond before finishing.

Basin Stone

STOODLEY PIKE

*An exhilarating and easy high-level march on the Lumbutts
and Mankinholes skyline to a celebrated Pennine landmark*

START *Lumbutts (SD 945231; OL14 6JJ)*

DISTANCE *5³⁄4 miles (9¹⁄4km)*

ORDNANCE SURVEY 1:25,000 MAP
Explorer OL21 - South Pennines

ACCESS *Start from the Shepherd's Rest Inn a short mile west
of Lumbutts. Roadside parking on approach from Lumbutts
(pub car park is for patrons only). Bus from Todmorden.*

The Shepherd's Rest occupies a splendid position on a road
summit high above Todmorden: the monument on Stoodley Pike is
in view from the outset. From a gate opposite the pub, a broad
path bears left across the moorland of Langfield Common.
Immediately crossing a splendid flagged packhorse route, a minute
further a fork is reached: keep to the gentler left branch to rise
steadily across the moor. *Throughout this rolling moorland section
vast, sweeping views look across upper Calderdale, full of colour
and interest, with the Stoodley Pike monument a near permanent
beacon ahead.* The path rises ever gradually beneath shapely rock
formations and scars of long abandoned quarrying on the cliffs of
Langfield Edge. Your improving path is carried across successive
embankments of two old dams beneath former quarries.

Eventually this splendidly engineered way gains the far end of the brooding rocks, then a path contours around the head of deep-cut Black Clough. Doubling back across the far side, it is now set back from the clough. The path remains clear as it bears right and commences a gentle rise above very modest Noon Stone Edge enhanced by a rash of boulders. As the slope tails off so do the rocks, and the path skirts the mound of Coldwell Hill on your right. *Withens Clough Reservoir appears to the east.* Faced with a group of boulders the path drops gently right to merge with the infallible course of the Pennine Way. Bear left on its part-flagged course past a memorial seat on a short stony drop to a dip. Ignoring an early lesser branch curving right, rise to a crossroads with a well-preserved paved way.

The junction is overseen by the Long Stoop, a very old guidepost of quite monumental stature. *Here the Pennine Way, the modern traveller's highway, meets a centuries-old pack-horse route known (like a number of*

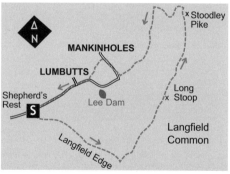

others) as the Long Causeway. The preserved section of flags can be seen going all the way down towards Mankinholes. Your path advances straight on, rising past boulders on the left through an old quarry and following a broad and popular level course past clusters of rocks along to the Stoodley Pike monument.

Erected in 1815 to celebrate peace after victory over Napoleon, it later collapsed and was replaced by a new tower in 1856. An inscription over the door explains some of its history. It stands a mighty 120 feet above the 1312ft/400m moortop, and is the upper valley's most famous landmark. A dark, spiral staircase climbs 39 steps to a viewing balcony: the 360-degree panorama features moorland skylines in almost every direction, while an intriguing aspect is the way intervening plateaux largely mask the industrialised valley floor.

Leave by a broad path departing the edge just a few yards west of the monument. This drops briefly away then slants left across the steep slopes, before long turning sharp right, and forking. Take the right option, dropping down a short groove to merge with another path, and go right down this to drop pleasantly onto a broad, firm bridle-path along the foot of the moor. *The modern housing of Harvelin Park directly below occupies the site of two Victorian hospitals that only closed in 1987. The Fielden Hospital of 1892 largely catered for infectious diseases and later children, while Stansfield View Hospital of 1879 began life as Todmorden Poor Law Union Workhouse, and later devoted to mental health.* Turning left, it runs a largely level course beneath the Pike's steep slopes. This old track known as London Road leads unfailingly along the foot of the common to eventually reach a corner. Through the gate ahead a walled track runs on to drop down to the edge of Mankinholes. *Alongside is a nice floral corner featuring two stone sheep, a Millennium stone and a seat.*

Turn right through the intriguing hamlet. *Passing through this old handloom weaving settlement you passing impressive water troughs recalling its importance in packhorse days, and a surviving youth hostel in a fine old building.* Beyond the last buildings you quickly reach a lone house. *This is a former Wesleyan Methodist Sunday School of 1833, the chapel itself being demolished in 1979: alongside is a burial ground.* Here turn left down the splendidly paved Lumbutts Lane to emerge at the Top Brink Inn at Lumbutts. *At the very foot of the lane note an old guidepost inscribed 'Halifax' and 'Heptonstall', complete with mileages.* With the pub to your left, go straight ahead down an enclosed, setted path the short way onto the road by an old tower.

The attractive settlement of Lumbutts nestles in a hollow dominated by a former water wheel tower. This immense structure once contained three vertically arranged wheels, each fed from above as well as independently. It served a cotton mill that once stood here. Immediately above the tower is Lee Dam, one of three tree-shrouded dams hovering above the hamlet and the scene of an annual New Year 'dip' - for the brave or foolhardy! Turn right through the hamlet and head along the long, rising road back to the start. *En route note a sundial of 1864 on the corner of a cottage, complete with a 'time-rhyme'.*

BLACKSTONE EDGE

Largely easy moorland walking to a landmark crest

START *Windy Hill (SD 983141; OL3 5UN)*

DISTANCE *6¼ miles (10km)*

ORDNANCE SURVEY 1:25,000 MAP
Explorer OL21 - South Pennines

ACCESS *Start from a parking area amid boundary signs by large mast on A672 half-mile west of Junction 22 of M62. Halifax-Rochdale bus. • OPEN ACCESS: includes water company permissive paths within Open Access land, see page 8.*

Despite the remoteness of this walk, the dominant feature is the presence of man, be it reservoir, pylon, motorway, Roman road, packway, mast, windfarm, ... Also novel is the starting altitude at an appropriately blustery 1368ft/417m up! A more historic Milnrow/Rishworth boundary stone stands amid modern signs, and from the outset Blackstone Edge beckons beyond the mast. From the parking area follow the firm course of the Pennine Way northwards, crossing the mast access road and dropping down, part flagged, to quickly reach the Pennine Way footbridge. *You are now the highest person in the country 'on' a motorway.*

Across, bear left on the stony path rising to a cairned knoll, then on to a bridle-gate in a fence. *Here you leave Yorkshire for under two miles until just beyond the Aiggin Stone.* The path swings around to the right to replace the M62 with the prospect of Blackstone Edge, a fair deal! The restored path makes light work of the once intimidating peat bogs of Redmires as old mill flagstones saunter through the cotton-grass. Across the head of Longden End Clough the path rises towards the edge. The flagstones end and Green Withens Reservoir appears in its entirety down to the right - you will later return along its embankment. With the bouldery crest of the edge straight ahead, the path passes a circular stone shelter just before veering left to finally gain the crest between minor peat groughs. It is now a brief stroll to the waiting Ordnance Survey column to the right.

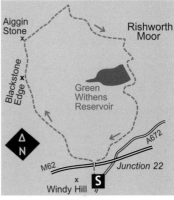

The trig point at 1548ft/472m is cemented onto a mighty boulder top, although the high point would appear to be the immediately previous boulders. Windfarms aplenty feature in a very expansive view. Westwards you look down onto a great spread of greater Manchester beyond Littleborough and Hollingworth Lake. Summit Gorge is backed by Scout Moor, leading the eye to Pendle Hill through the Cliviger Gorge, while to the north are Black Hameldon and Boulsworth Hill. Southwards are the high moors of the Dark Peak. Perhaps the finest feature is the rocky edge itself: the finest climbing ground amongst what is otherwise largely scrambling opportunities is found towards the northern limits of the edge, and set a short way down the slope.

Resume northwards along the edge path, soon dropping gently down, leaving the 'edge' behind and running pleasantly along to soon arrive at a bridle-gate admitting onto a path junction presided over by a colourful guidepost at the Aiggin Stone. *This is a junction of once-important packhorse routes, where Rochdale-Halifax and Oldham-Burnley trails met. The old guidestone has been restored, and remarkably there is more of it below ground than above. Further down on the Lancashire side is a superb surviving setted section, long attributed to the Romans but probably dating from packhorse times.* Turn right, the path immediately crossing the brow and soon diverging from the fence. A gradual descent begins on a varied but clear, distinctive part-sunken way, a little peaty in parts. *The modern path runs slightly to the north of the original route. Baitings Reservoir is ahead beneath Great Manshead Hill.* The path drops down to a wooden footbridge on the concrete Rishworth Drain, across which a grassy path is met.

Turn right on the inviting drain-side path, quickly curving left at a gate in the fence met earlier: the drain runs marginally uphill to reach a 'nick' in the moor. *This reveals the moors to the south joining the Windy Hill mast.* A grassy path comes in from the left, and across a drain bridge, the Rishworth Drain goes off right. Here leave it by rising onto the minor brow in front, revealing the motor-way ahead. Now bear left on a good path forming alongside yet another reedy drain. *Green Withens Reservoir appears below, with the crest of Blackstone Edge back to the right.* The way runs on, rising gently towards Green Withens Edge. Shortly after a small, bracken-draped clough, you reach the abrupt end of the drain. Here the path bears right a few paces then turns distinctly down the moor, descending alongside bracken on your left. A guidepost at the start of a brief reedy section indicates the arrival of a lesser path from the right: your briefly thinner continuation bears left through the reeds to quickly improve as it crosses grassy moor to a wide bridge over a major drain. Turn right on the broad track to quickly reach a valve house by the dam of Green Withens Reservoir. *En route note the modest remains of an iron track in the path, a survivor from the reservoir's construction.*

Beyond the outflow a splendid grassy stroll shadows the dam wall above the rough road, leading around two sides to a water-sports centre on the other side. *All the while, Blackstone Edge still features prominently across the rising moor beyond the reservoir head. Green Withens Reservoir was completed in 1898 by Wakefield Corporation, and enlarged in 1925.* Go left on the stony drive out, again with a drain for company. When the reservoir road turns off for the main road, keep right on a grassy path by the drain to reach its terminus at a concrete basin under the motorway fence. A broad path turns up its side to quickly return you to the motorway footbridge, to conclude as you began.

HARDCASTLE CRAGS

Woodland and moor-edge tracks above Crimsworth Dean

START *Midgehole (SD 988291; HX7 7AL)*

DISTANCE *6 miles (9^{1}2km)*

ORDNANCE SURVEY 1:25,000 MAP
Explorer OL21 - South Pennines

ACCESS *Start from National Trust car park/WC at New Bridge, main car park for Hardcastle Crags off A6033 Keighley road out of Hebden Bridge. Summer weekend bus from Hebden Bridge.*

Hardcastle Crags is the name by which everyone knows Hebden Dale, through which flows Hebden Water. The majority of this beautifully wooded dale is in the National Trust's care. From the bottom car park head up the drive a few strides until just past a lodge, then fork left on a path descending to Hebden Water. Here a wide path is met and accompanied upstream for almost a mile and a half to Gibson Mill. The first of two impasses is quickly reached as the path slants back up right a little to run a parallel course above the beck. Soon forking, one drops back to the beck to return a little later, or you could simply remain on this level one higher above the bank. Having merged, the path now runs on to quickly drop back to the beck to commence a delectable stroll upstream. Further, the path is forced slightly up again in two near parallel sections, to run on again a little higher to soon reach a T-

23

junction: drop left the short way to a clearing at stepping-stones. From here an unbroken stroll leads upstream to the mill, passing further stepping-stones. A 'psalm plaque' adorns a rock in the beck as the mill appears ahead.

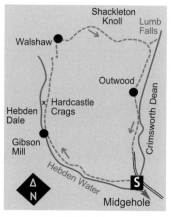

Gibson Mill was founded in 1800 as a water-powered cotton mill known as Lord Holme Mill. It ceased to operate in the 1890s, becoming a dance hall and a roller-skating rink during the mid-20th century – known as the Entertainment Emporium. This well-preserved building has a cafe, shop, information and exhibitions. Now at the very forefront of sustainable 21st century technology, it produces its own power by solar and water. Related features include a row of workers' cottages, while a stone-arched bridge spans the beck to WCs. Around the back is a millpond. Join the adjacent driveway to climb above the beck, within a few minutes reaching a branch path signed left to 'The Crags'. This demands a splendid short detour winding up onto the pronounced spur, quickly ascending to the steep rise of Hardcastle Crags. *This grouping of modest rock outcrops occupies a prominent knoll bedecked with clumps of heather, with a slender ridge rising above the treetops.*

Continuing, simply remain on the main drive to a fork where it swings more sharply uphill. Here take the less firm, more inviting level cart track running left, enjoying a super contour along the wooded flanks, and shortly dropping almost to beck level. Immediately on crossing a footbridge on Rowshaw Clough, take a less obvious path slanting right through a gateway in an old wall. It climbs steeply above the stream, remaining close to it as other branches go left. At the wood top go left a few strides to a small gate into a field, then ascend the wall then fence side with the imposing Walshaw Lodge just above. To the right of the lodge a tiny enclosure is entered by a gate and left by a corner stile a little higher, putting you into the yard of this farming hamlet. *This ancient settlement features an 1860s shooting lodge to the left, whose impressive front boasts an enviable view down-dale.*

Rise right a few paces to a track junction, and turn right on the main access road leaving the hamlet. Almost at once leave by a gate on the left, which sends a walled track away. This soon becomes unenclosed to cross to a tiny beck and a gate. It then rises round the top of a much larger pasture, fading but remaining with the top wall almost to the far corner. Here a bridle-gate transfers you onto open moor, and a broad wallside path contours to the right beneath Shackleton Knoll. *At 1214ft/370m the walk's high point is reached: ubiquitous features of the view are Heptonstall church tower and Stoodley Pike.* As the environs of Crimsworth Dean are approached, the moor is vacated at a gate to descend a walled green track, Coppy Lane, to a junction at ruinous Nook.

Go right just a couple of strides on the track, and resume your steep descent by a streamlet towards the valley floor. Rough slopes lead down to merge into an old walled way, and down to the ruin of Sunny Bank just below. From here an improved enclosed path slants left with a streamlet down to a path junction on a knoll. You shall resume right from here, but first take a couple of minutes to slant left down the path to view the immediately revealed Lumb Bridge and Lumb Hole waterfall on Crimsworth Dean Beck. *This is a delectable scene of packhorse bridge and delightful falls.*

Return to the junction and as your previous path climbs steeply right, pass through an old gateway in front onto a narrower path. Remaining parallel with the beck, the path contours delightfully through several bracken-filled pastures, eventually encountering a sturdy wall-stile at the end. Passing to the rear of the humble dwelling of Outwood follow its grassy drive to reach a gate into National Trust woodland. Ignore this however in favour of a gap to its left, and a part-flagged path slants down across the field to a stile into the woods. A path runs down to the stone-arched Weet Ing Bridge. Don't cross but continue on the same bank, rising a little then running towards a gate into a field. Just 100 yards before it however, rise half-right on a thinner but clear path slanting up to join the main drive. This is followed left all the way back down to Midgehole, ignoring any branches. Beyond an old quarry a firmer access road comes in. Into trees this becomes surfaced at Hollin Hall for the final stage back to the start.

WALSHAW DEAN

A good mix of heather moorland and colourful valley lead to a necklace of reservoirs in a fold of the hills

START Widdop (SD 947323; HX7 7AT)

DISTANCE $6\frac{3}{4}$ miles ($10\frac{3}{4}$km)

ORDNANCE SURVEY 1:25,000 MAP
Explorer OL21 - South Pennines

ACCESS Start from a roadside parking area opposite Gorple water company road just east of Clough Foot, half a mile west of Pack Horse inn on Heptonstall-Colne road.
• OPEN ACCESS: The permissive path from Walshaw to Walshaw Dean may be closed on certain days during the grouse shooting season and at times of high fire risk. An alternative route is available. Dogs must be on leads from March to July.

From the lay-by follow the road south-east towards the well-named pub, also known as The Ridge. However, beyond a lone house a bridle-gate on the right gives access to a short-lived green way. At the end go left with a crumbling wall along the edge of the deep little clough. After an intervening stile the path quickly bears away from the wall to immediately fork above the narrow valley of Graining Water. Keep straight on by the wall with some scattered boulders below. *A bend in the old wall and some rocks is the place to look down on a lovely watersmeet, with Lower Gorple's grassy dam immediately behind.* The little path forges on with old wall and fence, and in time the old wall departs and the fence becomes more distant. The path continues a delightful level course through scattered rocks and some bracken. As the more imposing gritstone outcrops of Ridge Scout appear, the path starts a splendid, gentle descent, slanting into denser bracken and down beneath the largest group of outcrops to a gate in a fence. Just a few strides further is a stile onto a hairpin bend of the road.

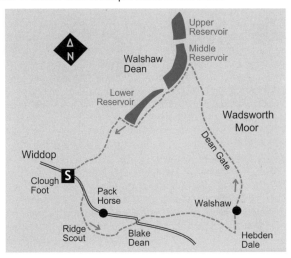

The building in front is on the site of a Baptist Chapel of 1802: the burial ground survives. Turn downhill, and leave by a gateway on the left between a driveway and Blake Dean Bridge. A path drops down a few stone steps and along the short way to a footbridge on Alcomden Water in Blake Dean. *This local beauty spot features a colourful watersmeet with grassy banks and green islands beneath steep slopes.* Take the main path climbing away, and when a broad green path comes along from an old railway cutting, turn right on it. *Shortly, down below, five footings can clearly be seen by the stream. These supported a 700ft/215m long trestle viaduct which carried a railway 100ft/30m above the beck, constructed in 1901 to transport materials to Walshaw Dean reservoir site.*

On reaching a stile, a slimmer path runs on through bracken and low crags, and through an old wall into woodland. Very quickly nearing an open field above, bear left to the wall corner just ahead, and a short way along it the path passes through the old wall to resume along the colourful field bottom. At the end the path advances the short way to the isolated house at Over Wood. Its access track takes over to head into deeper woods at the head of Hebden Dale, working its way gradually towards the valley floor beneath bluebell slopes.

After about ten minutes a bridge is reached at a sidestream: without advancing to the path junction just across it, turn left up a narrow path immediately before the stream. It rises through an old gateway on the left and climbs steeply above the stream in Rowshaw Clough, remaining close to it as other branches go left. At the wood top go left a few strides to a small gate into a field, then rise towards Walshaw shooting lodge. *With its enviable view down-dale, it dates from the 1860s, part of an attractive and ancient farming hamlet.* To the right of the lodge a tiny enclosure is entered by a gate, with a corner stile just above putting you into the yard. The enclosed track rising directly from the top end is your route, assuming there are no signs to the contrary. *If there should be, then turn left on the broad track between the buildings, and it runs unerringly on to rejoin the main route near the end.*

On heading up the track, leave it as soon as it turns sharp left to New Cote Farm, immediately after another drive has gone right. A little path branches off up a small tract of open ground. Rejoining a track at a gate just above, this ascends the wallside to become enclosed at the top. It rises pleasantly to emerge via a stile/gate onto a corner of Wadsworth Moor. Ignoring the track, ascend a narrow path to quickly meet the track again at a fork. Take the left branch straight ahead, effortlessly ascending the moor to the walk's summit at some 1380ft/420m. *Known as Dean Gate, this pleasant path is now a Landrover track. Sweeping views look out over heather-clad moors to Gorple Upper, Lower and Widdop reservoirs to the left, with Black Hameldon and Boulsworth Hill on the high western skyline.* The descent towards Walshaw Dean sees all three of its reservoirs soon appear, one by one. A short way beneath a stone shooting box is a fork: the left branch is slightly shorter, but the better route goes straight on down to a gate in a wall. Just beyond this it bridges a drain alongside Walshaw Dean Middle Reservoir. Here double back left on the Pennine Way which runs a good course between drain and reservoir.

The trio of reservoirs occupying the floor of Walshaw Dean was begun in 1900 and the reservoirs officially opened in 1907, but leakage problems meant the job was only fully completed in 1915. With three reservoirs under construction the workforce peaked at more than 500 men, most accommodated at a lively shanty town nearby. At the end you bridge the drain to rejoin a track, but don't follow it across the dam to the former keeper's house. Instead go straight ahead on the Pennine Way, a firm, part flagged path running a generally level course beneath a sturdy wall above the full length of Walshaw Dean Lower Reservoir. Bridging the outflow at the end, cross the grassy embankment and briefly leave the track for a small gateway to the left, then up a fence-side path onto the surfaced reservoir road. Turning left this leads back to the start, avoiding a pair of left forks at a grassy triangle and passing a plantation. Dropping to a bend just before the road, a bridle-gate on the left cuts a small corner to gain the lay-by.

Ridge Scout

WALK 7 HEPTONSTALL

An iconic hilltop village sits amid swathes of interest

START *Hebden Bridge (SD 992273; HX7 8EX)*

DISTANCE *5³⁄4 miles (9¹⁄4km)*

ORDNANCE SURVEY 1:25,000 MAP
Explorer OL21 - South Pennines

ACCESS *Start from the old bridge on Bridge Gate in town centre. Car parks. Halifax-Todmorden bus and train; bus from Keighley.*

Hebden Bridge is the focal point of Upper Calderdale, its houses climbing alarmingly up steep hillsides above the meeting of two valleys. It is for here that most visitors make, partly for its position at the foot of Hebden Dale (Hardcastle Crags), but also for its own attractions. In the early 1970s this was a run-down mill town where houses could be picked up with loose change, but a hippy influx sowed the seeds for a remarkable transformation into the vibrant, arty hub you see today. The lively centre boasts canal trips, independent shops, a visitor centre at the marina on the Rochdale Canal, the Little Theatre, an iconic cinema, the Trades Club music venue and an arts festival in summer. The town was devastated by the Boxing Day floods of 2015.

From Bridge Gate cross the stone-arched packhorse bridge on Hebden Water and cross the road to The Buttress, a relentlessly steep cobbled old way. *With big views back over town it passes a*

Methodist burial ground near the top. Joining a level road, go left a few strides to an old milestone at a junction, then ascend an access road opposite. Beyond the second house it ends at a small quarry site. Just before it, a part enclosed path heads off right, rising gently through part wooded surrounds, curving around and up to emerge via the front of a short terrace onto a road at the foot of Heptonstall. Turn left up past the Post office/shop and tearoom.

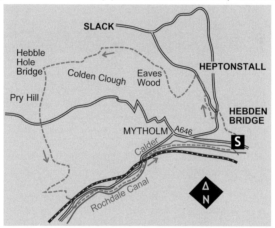

Heptonstall is a fascinating village steeped in history, of greater importance than Hebden Bridge until the arrival of the Industrial Revolution. Its exposed position defended on three sides by precipitous slopes has created a timewarp in which its weather-beaten stone cottages revel. Focal point is the churchyard which separates the imposing church of 1854 from the shell of the old church of St Thomas a'Becket, partly dating from the 13th century. The American poet/writer Sylvia Plath is buried here, as is David Hartley, leader of a notorious gang of 'coiners': he was executed in 1769 for his part in the murder of an exciseman who had come too close to uncovering their practice of clipping, melting down and creating counterfeit coins. Alongside is the old grammar school of 1772, now a museum. Seek out also the octagonal Wesleyan chapel (1764), the old dungeon (1824) and the 16th century Cloth Hall. There are two pubs, the Cross Inn and the White Lion.

Leave the main street by an enclosed path to the museum on the left, between the pubs. Passing the museum it enters the old churchyard. Advance to the new church, and a path goes left out onto a rough lane. Bear right on this, quickly crossing a suburban road. Just a little further at a fork, ignore the cart track bearing left and take the surfaced path bearing right. This runs between more gardens, over another road then escapes to emerge onto the crest of Eaves Wood. This reveals dramatic views from airy gritstone outcrops into Colden Clough: take care! *Stoodley Pike is seen from valley floor to towering monument.* Turn right on a splendid high-level path above the wooded clough. Keeping to the upper path, the later stages feature a gentle clamber through the bouldery wood top before joining an access road, Green Lane. Turn down this a short way, and at old troughs take a level path striking right.

This meets another rising from the left, and together rising to a small open area where several paths meet. Go straight ahead to a wall-stile right of a seat, and head directly away on a stone-flagged path. Over a stile at the end, pass the house on your left and ascend its driveway very briefly. As it bends right, take the enclosed path dropping left. Quickly forking on open ground, take the right branch which runs along a field top. Continue through small gates at the end and flagstones re-appear. From a gate at the end resume with a wall on your left, quickly reaching a kink where the causey passes through a stile to slant diagonally down to a stile into Foster Wood. The old way resumes to the right along the wood top, and on dropping to reach another junction slant left down to Hebble Hole Bridge. *This 300-year old clapper bridge consists of two sets of stone slabs in a charming location on Colden Water, part of an old traders' way linking Blackshaw Head and Heptonstall.*

Across the bridge take the PW rising steeply left up the heather bank, mostly stone-stepped to gain a firm track along the top. From a stile opposite ascend the deeply enclosed footway for some time, finally emerging into a field at a bridle-gate. Maintain this rise up the fieldside, through another and then a third one takes you over the brow of Pry Hill. *Leaving Colden Clough behind, ahead is Stoodley Pike across the main valley.* Drop down to a stile onto a road, Badger Lane, and cross straight over down a short drive-way. As it swings left to the house, take a stile in front and descend the outer garden edge to a small gate into a field. Drop down with the wall on your right, and when it ends continue down to pick up another wall. Continue down to a kissing-gate and the few steps further down to a stile onto another access road, Winter's Lane.

Go briefly left to the first house, after which take the access road branching down to the right. This slants down to quickly arrive at further scattered houses. Look out for a PW sign immediately after a house on the right sending you to the start of an enclosed setted path. This drops right through a gap then steeply down beneath a stone shed into the top of a wood. The super path now slants right down through scattered trees, with the wood floor rich in springtime bluebells. Reaching a junction bear right, resuming the slant down to a gate/stile onto an access road.

Double back left, dropping down to quickly reach a further house and fork. The way drops right down setted Nabby Lane until just past a white house on your left. Here take a narrow path dropping right, steeply down and setted between walls to the next house, where it bears right along the front then steeply down again to emerge between tall houses at Lacy House. Go straight ahead on Underbank Avenue, beneath the railway arch and out onto the A646. Go briefly right on the footway to a pedestrian crossing, over

which follow an access road over the River Calder to the Rochdale Canal towpath. Turn left to return to Hebden Bridge. *Features en route include several locks and an 'island' spell as the river comes in on your left: steep woods hang above the canal. Almost at the end is the Stubbing Wharf pub and Hebble End, with art studios and a cafe.* The canal is left alongside a bridge to drop left onto Holme Street, emerging in the centre.

*St Thomas a'Becket,
Heptonstall*

SCAMMONDEN WATER

Reservoirs and moorland by the M62, with sweeping views

START *Booth Wood (SE 031165; HX6 4RH)*

DISTANCE *5^{1}4 miles (8^{1}2km)*

ORDNANCE SURVEY 1:25,000 MAP
Explorer OL21 - South Pennines

ACCESS *Start from Yorkshire Water's Booth Wood Reservoir car park on A672, half-mile south of Rishworth. Permissive paths.*

Booth Wood Reservoir was built in 1971, and the car park sits by its mighty concrete dam, with the M62 motorway just across it. To the west is the Turnpike Inn, while to the east above Rishworth is Booth Wood Inn. A clear path leaves the bottom end of the car park, briefly parallel with the road before dropping down wooden steps onto an abandoned road. *This was the A672 until nudged onto its present course by the reservoir.* Go briefly left to Moselden Lane, and turn right down it. Swinging down beneath the dam, as it doubles back left above the head of Booth Dean Clough, take a stile on the right. A path climbs steeply through trees to join a road. Cross to a kissing-gate above, and a grassy path ascends open ground to rejoin the access road just short of the motorway.

Rise through the eastbound underpass to an unsurfaced fork. *The right branch makes for Stott Hall Farm, famous for retaining its isolated position in the middle of the motorway.* Take the left branch, rising to the westbound underpass before turning right to run parallel with the motorway. *The M62 trans-Pennine motorway was first conceived in 1961, and ten years later traffic was tracing its graceful lines over the Yorkshire-Lancashire watershed. The engineering achievement that earned greatest recognition was the bridging of the Scammonden valley, a project that took over three years to complete. With a reservoir planned around the same time, logical consensus was that the two could combine to serve each other's needs. Thus it was that a larger dam than initially conceived, some 249ft high, would span the valley and carry the motorway towards its summit four miles to the west.*

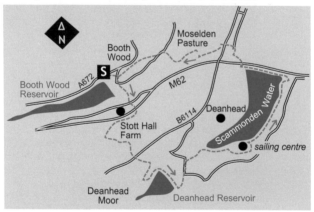

Further on, the track bears left with a wall to a barn beneath the old farm of High Moss. Pass the barn to a gate/stile from where the track becomes briefly enclosed. At the end ignore the gate and use a gateway to its left, then head away on a rougher green track ascending moor-grass slopes with a wall on your right. Quickly passing through another gateway, double back left to rise with a wall. An improving path follows a reedy wallside ditch, and when the ditch ends a continuing path ascends to a brow. *Massive views look back over the motorway.* The little path runs on with the wall to fade as the wall turns off, but with fences either side a track runs the short way to a stile/gate onto the B6114 Saddleworth Road. *At around 1256ft/383m this is the summit of the walk.*

A thin path heads away from a stile/gate opposite, quickly bringing both Scammonden Water and Deanhead Reservoir into the scene in the valley below. *Scammonden is well wooded, Deanhead sits amid remote moors.* The path runs to a crumbling wall corner, and descends with it. Halfway down, take the path slanting left to a small gate in a fence. Don't use it but double back right, slanting down above the fence to meet a wall at a grooved path coming in from the left. Follow this slanting gently right, down to a junction of old ways in front of long abandoned Upper Gate Head. Double back left down another hollowed way to the remains of Lower Gate Head. A thin trod follows an old wall to a sturdy wall-stile. Just beyond, you meet a track at Deanhead Reservoir's embankment.

Cross the stile/gate and follow the grassy embankment path. *The reservoir was completed in 1836 to supply textile mills: across it are the cloughs and folds of Deanhead Moor. Note the tapestry of field walls on the northern slopes, not an intact one among them as water interests ensured farming took second place. Down valley the motorway crosses Scammonden's embankment.* Having bridged the outflow take the rough road down to a stile/gate onto New Lane, and turn left down to a car park. Passing through into the recreation area alongside, a firm path runs along the bottom to enter trees alongside Black Burne Brook. Ignore an early footbridge and keep on to quickly reach the head of Scammonden Water.

The path runs pleasantly by the shore to soon reach an impasse at a slipway. A stiff pull right quickly joins an access road: go left the short way towards a scouts' activity centre. Without entering, take a broad path slanting right through colourful surrounds. Within a couple of minutes fork left to a bridle-gate above the sailing clubhouse at the old vicarage. *St Bartholomew's church at Deanhead is seen across the water from numerous stages.* A little further it drops steeply back to the shore, resuming above the bank for a sustained stroll. Ignoring a right branch uphill at an early fork, continue to a fork with an underpass visible just ahead. *A tablet by the valve tower at the end proclaims the lake's opening by the Queen in 1971.* Bear right, climbing briefly steeply to meet a level path. Go left on this to quickly arrive at the end of the embankment, and cross the dam on a broad path just a fence away from the waggons.

At the far end don't follow the surfaced path ahead, but drop left a few yards to leave in favour of an underpass on your right.

Emerging at the other side of the motorway, a broad track rises briefly left. *Pause to admire the brand new view down Black Brook valley beneath the motorway and enormous grass embankment.* The tarmac track quickly turns to climb steeply right to the terminus of Lower Road. Go briefly right past a few houses, but leave by the walled green path of Pill Box Lane on the left before a house. This quickly rises to meet the B6114 Saddleworth Road again.

Go left just 50 yards and turn right on a hard track rising into recolonised ground, with trees to the right. At a junction before the brow take the slimmer, surfaced path running left to a fence high above the motorway. It turns right with it to a brow, but as it turns right again, keep on to drop to a fence-stile into Moselden Pasture. *Dramatic views look ahead to a big spread of Saddleworth Moor, the motorway, Booth Wood Reservoir, Blackstone Edge and Rishworth Moor.* A thin path drops directly away with the fence on your left, fading just before crossing a slight old wall to reach a ramshackle fence meeting the motorway fence. Negotiate this and drop to a rough service road for the mast below. Follow this right to a junction on a sharp bend, and go left to drop untidily towards an isolated house at Broad Ing. *You could go right on the inviting grassy embankment of the drain, and on reaching a stone-arched bridge double back left down a short path onto this track.*

Just before drawing level with the house, escape right down a rough pasture, just short of a fence. As the fence disappears, traces of an old wall point you down to a fence-stile onto Moselden Lane. Go very briefly left to a minor dip, and take a stile/gate on the right. Beyond a metal hut an improving path slants gently down above the scattered trees of Booth Dean Clough. At the bottom corner it drops to cross a wooden footbridge on a sidestream. A path runs on through trees to a near immediate fork: pass through the old stile ahead and stone steps drop you into a surprising corner where you cross Booth Dean Beck by a splendid, narrow stone-arched bridge. On the other side a tall-walled, stone-setted path runs the few yards to an old mill. *Abandoned by the passage of time, this is the charismatic ruin of Boothwood Paper Mills. A flight of 107 dank stone steps climb alongside it for an alternative finish by road.* Pass through a gap alongside the mill from where a path heads upstream through trees. This leads pleasantly along to a stile back onto Moselden Lane near the start, to retrace opening steps.

UPPER RYBURN

An intimate exploration of the uppermost Ryburn Valley

START Ripponden (SE 040197; HX6 4DF)

DISTANCE 5³4 miles (9¹4km)

ORDNANCE SURVEY 1:25,000 MAP
Explorer OL21 - South Pennines

ACCESS Start from the village centre. Royd Lane car park above main road. Bus from Halifax via Sowerby Bridge.

Ripponden is a busy village, its old centre being a conservation area. Here St Bartholomew's church spire reaches to the heavens, alongside a restored packhorse bridge leading to the white-walled and even more historic Old Bridge Inn. Further pubs, shops and a cafe are close by. The railway arrived from Sowerby Bridge in 1881 and closed in 1958: sections are put to use as permissive paths. From the church do not cross either of the bridges, but pass between the houses of Mill Fold at Bridge End and underneath the main road bridge over the River Ryburn. *The Ryburn flows around seven miles from the high moors beneath Blackstone Edge to join the Calder at Sowerby Bridge.*

A setted road heads upstream, then you pass through a small park onto a road. Advance along its riverside course, and beyond houses and a small industrial site a surfaced drive runs along the riverbank. When this ends at Ellis Bottom Farm a path takes over to trace the Ryburn to a footbridge. *This woodland section is superb: across the river is modern housing on the site of former mills, though several weirs testify to the traditional mill needs of times past: the most action they see today is a heron taking flight.* Don't cross, but take a few stone steps up to resume through the trees. Ignore too a branch left up to an old bridge over the former railway. The path drops back to the Ryburn and on above a steep plunge to the river to reach a confluence. Just to the left the inflowing Booth Dean Beck leads you to a road, the short-lived Holme House Lane. Turn right to bridge the beck up onto the A672 at Slitheroe Bridge. *The branch line from Sowerby Bridge ended here, at Rishworth station.*

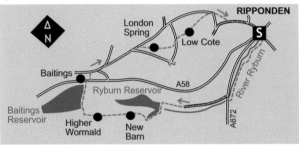

Use the main road to cross the Ryburn and depart immediately left on Bar Lane, parallel with the river. This runs upstream to an eventual demise at new housing on the site of a mill. *Latterly a paper mill, a nice touch into the 1990s was a quaint fire appliance in its own garage.* En route much housing is passed, then a millpond on the left and an almost hidden one on the right. A setted road takes over to climb to a hairpin bend: here pass to the left of a tumbledown garage, where a path is found with a millpond below and the dam of Ryburn Reservoir dramatically in front. Continuing up, steps climb to emerge at a car park at the dam's north end. *Ryburn Reservoir was built in 1933 for Wakefield Corporation, and largely surrounded by woodland, even with its curved concrete dam it blends well in its deep fold of the valley. This is in contrast to its more recent neighbour, whose dam is visible ahead. Beneath Ryburn's dam compare 'progress' in water conservation, with the old millpond overshadowed by the hundred foot high dam.*

Cross the dam and take the broad path to the right, above the water's edge to reach a footbridge over the head of the reservoir's southern arm. Across it a path climbs through trees to a stile into a field, then rises by a wall to become enclosed before arriving at New Barn Farm. An enclosed path passes right of the buildings, through an outer yard to a small gate. It resumes enclosed directly along the field behind, through a bridle-gate to rise alongside a wall then fence. Soon levelling out, this straight line runs to a stile, and becomes enclosed. *Across to the left is the wide span of Rishworth Moor, while Baitings Dam re-appears beneath Manshead End.* Continue along this pleasant crest, and just beyond a gap-stile the way kinks slightly to the right and begins to rise away. As the old way swings up to the left, take a small gate on the right into a field containing the ruin of once substantial New House just down to the right.

From the wall corner by the ruin its grassy former access track runs left, rising gently with a wall in the direction of Baitings Reservoir. It soon becomes enclosed to run pleasantly on to the house at Higher Wormald, with a 1796 datestone. At the end don't follow the drive rising away, but take a kissing-gate by the out-house on the right to cross two fields to Upper Schole Carr Farm. Turn right down a track to cross the dam of Baitings Reservoir. *This was completed as recently as 1956 on the site of a much smaller reservoir dating from the 1920s. The massive concrete dam might rapidly induce vertigo, being curiously sinuous and with unusually low walls. Hold on to your false teeth if peering over it!*

Across the dam cross a car park to join the A58. *The house to the left was, into the 21st century, the New Inn, sporting a large sundial of 1764.* From a stile opposite a path climbs outside the garden edge, over an intervening stile to rise to a stile onto the parallel Blue Ball Road. *Disaster strikes again here as the house in front was, again until relatively recently, the once very popular Blue Ball Inn. Its reputation for its choice of good ales wasn't enough to save this old packhorse inn serving the route out of Lancashire over Blackstone Edge proper. This was superseded by the modern turnpike road over Blackstone Edge which adopted the lower route by what was the Blue Ball's suitably named lower neighbour. All that remains is its extensive view over the dam to Rishworth Moor.* Turn right along the quiet, level road (avoiding lesser turns) for a good three-quarters of a mile. At a crossroads with rough lanes just beyond a T-junction, go right on the walled track known as London Spring Road. Continue straight past the house at London Spring Farm, becoming a nicer track passing a pocket moor before running on to another road, Green Lane.

Go left just a few yards before branching right down another walled track, Cote Road. *Soon on the left you pass the splendid old house of Low Cote, with its mullioned windows and dainty gabled porch.* Further, a firm driveway comes in to run on to another road. *Just two minutes along to the right is the Beehive Inn, though Ripponden itself is only ten minutes away now.* Cross straight over behind a house, over a second road and along an enclosed cart track. When it turns sharp left just past a house, advance on over open ground. Just down the wallside a narrow green path soon becomes tightly enclosed by walls to descend to similarly narrow Royd Lane at a pleasant row of cottages. *A 1764 datestone adorns the next house down.* Royd Lane leads steeply and rapidly down into the centre of Ripponden. For the parish church cross straight over the main road and down a short lane to the Old Bridge Inn and packhorse bridge.

Baitings Dam from Upper Schole Carr

CRAGG VALE

Moderately strenuous walking from woodland to moorland

START *Mytholmroyd (SE 012260; HX7 5DS)*

DISTANCE *6 miles (9$\frac{1}{2}$km)*

ORDNANCE SURVEY 1:25,000 MAP
Explorer OL21 - South Pennines

ACCESS *Start from the village centre. Small car park over bridge at T-junction. Halifax-Hebden Bridge bus and train.*

Mytholmroyd sprang up with the textile mills, and now large pockets of modern housing extend around the valley. 'Royd' has the Dusty Miller pub, shops and cafes, while St Michael's church stands across the river where Cragg Brook joins the Calder. This is the birthplace of Ted Hughes (1930-1998), who became Poet Laureate in 1984. Such is the reputation of local dock leaves that the World Dock Pudding Championship is held here. Cross the bridge on the B6138 (with parallel footbridge), along New Road passing under the railway bridge. *On the left is a modern Roman Catholic church.* Opposite the Shoulder of Mutton (with mounting steps) bear left on Scout Road. *On the left stands the attractive 17th century Mytholmroyd Farmhouse.* At once turn sharply right up Hall Bank Lane at the side of a former Methodist church.

Ignoring suburban branches, remain on the steeply climbing lane to make a quick exit from town to country. *Looking over*

Mytholmroyd to the rolling moors behind, Heptonstall's church is conspicuous on the skyline, while Bell House Moor and Broadhead Clough impress over Cragg Vale. The road winds up to suddenly end as a drive goes left. Your continuation of Stake Lane is the broad, enclosed path ahead, climbing partly flagged and through colourful vegetation. Part way up leave at a gate/stile on the right, and a grassy path runs on the wallside beneath myriad hollies. Halfway along, slant left up a grassy way rising to level ground, then cross to a stone hut. To its left a broader, stony path slants up through scattered trees, then an open slope to a gate at the top.

Don't use the gate, but take a path on the right for a grand walk along the top of Hollin Hey Wood. At the end you emerge into more open country. *Revealed now are outstanding views over Cragg Vale: finest features are the wealth of woodland and the prospect of the wooded bowl of*

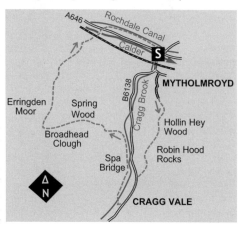

Broadhead Clough opposite, your return route. The path advances to a welcome bench above a rash of crags. Just past here it dips down, and the main path slants down to the right. *Just ahead a thinner path continues onto the crest of Robin Hood Rocks.*

Your descending path quickly swings left, and avoiding lesser branches fork left for a short, level grassy stroll to a stile out of the wood. A faint path crosses the field to the gateway ahead, but then turn down the nearside of the wall to a gate/stile. Continue on a clear path down by colourful vegetation to the edge of the wood, then bear left down a stone-flagged, walled way to a row of houses at Upper Birks in Cragg Vale. Turn down to the right here, and at the houses below drop left down onto the B6138 Cragg Road. Cross and go left on its broad footway past the Robin Hood pub. After further terraces bear right on a surfaced access road the few strides to Castlegate Mill, a pair of houses. Here take a path doubling back sharply right along the front, running a firm course through trees down onto a rough access road by Cragg Brook. *Remains of old mills both upstream and downstream include a waterwheel.*

Cross the bridge to Papermill Cottage, and from a gate on the right a broad path rises away, soon levelling out to run high above steep Papermill Wood. The left-hand wall soon disappears to leave you amid graceful beeches. Very shortly fork right down towards the brook, and from a kissing-gate cross two narrow equestrian paddocks. Emerging onto a drive, go down it to Spa Bridge just below. Steps lead down its near side to Cragg Spa. *A small spring enters a basin just a few feet from the river, and is thought to have been used at least 300 years ago for the supposed benefits of its sulphurous waters: at one time 'Spaw Sunday' celebrations took place on the first Sunday in May.* Without crossing the tall-arched bridge take a stile to resume downstream on a permissive path. A lovely wooded walk leads to Clough Foot Bridge. Just up to the left a gate/stile access a pasture, crossing it to a stile to resume downstream in woodland. The path soon swings left to a footbridge on a sidestream, then rises onto a drive. *For an easy return, turn right to Dauber Bridge, with the start half a mile distant along the road.*

For part two of the walk, turn left up the drive rising alongside the wooded clough. Leaving the stream it forks: bear left, running on to appraise the skyline of Broadhead Clough. Entering Spring Wood via a cattle-grid the drive forks: use neither, but take a much more inviting path straight ahead. *Here you enter Yorkshire Wildlife Trust's Broadhead Clough Nature Reserve.* Initially flagged, the path winds on and gradually upwards into the deep confines of this glorious woodland. A steep flight of wooden steps leads to easier progress and a super gentle ascent near this side of the wood. Shortly after a fence comes in on the right, you cross it via a kissing-gate from where the path climbs back to the right, and a surprise awaits as within a few feet it gains the rim of the amphitheatre on the edge of Erringden Moor. The climbing is over, and a tall stake serves as a useful waymark for those locating the path from above. *The great natural hollow of Broadhead Clough is also known locally as Bell Hole: this is truly a place to linger.*

Resume on a thin path heading directly away across the open moor, and from a crumbling wall corner the path runs a straight, near-level course alongside the faint vestiges of a wall. Evading some moist moments a wall corner is reached at the end. At this cross-paths head straight on with the wall on your right, skirting a marshy pool to another corner just ahead. *From the walk's high point at 1017ft/310km, note the landmark monument on Stoodley Pike breaking the moorland skyline to the left.* From this corner ideally leave the wall (and the faint continuing path ahead), and slant gently left (no path) to drop to a stile in the moor-bottom fence. Pass through the crumbling wall behind to start the long descent, the first section being alongside an old hollowed way known as Snail Lane. *The valley floor appears outspread below, with Mytholmroyd prominent, while hillside settlements such as Midgley and Heptonstall are also well seen.* The old way leads down to the grassy cart track of Haven Lane. Go right a few steps to a stile then resume the descent on a path slanting back to the left. This proves a splendid route down through colourful open country.

The path runs down towards a pylon, just beneath which it swings left towards the edge of trees. Along their fringe it turns downhill again, then slants right to a stile onto the access road of Wood Hey Lane, with houses a short way either side. From a stile opposite, a path drops down by a wooded stream. Through a stile at the bottom, drop down into a sheep pasture to a corner stile, beneath which is a slab bridge at a tiny confluence. Bear left across the field to a stile/gate in front of trees, joining a walled access lane.

This leads down to the right, keeping left past a fine old barn at Carr House. It becomes surfaced to cross railway and river to emerge onto the main road alongside a tall, redundant mill. *In the early 20th century this produced thousands of clog soles per week, and late that century became the popular retail outlet of Walkleys Clogs.* Cross the road with caution to join the towpath of the Rochdale Canal (see page 14), and turn right for a short walk back into Mytholmroyd. Passing Broadbottom Lock and beneath a couple of stone-arched bridges, leave the towpath at steps up onto a modern road bridge. Turn right down Midgley Road, with the walk's starting point just along to the right.

LUDDENDEN DEAN

An absorbing exploration of a hugely characterful valley

START *Luddenden (SE 041257; HX2 6PL)*

DISTANCE *6$\frac{3}{4}$ miles (10$\frac{3}{4}$km)*

ORDNANCE SURVEY 1:25,000 MAP
Explorer OL21 - South Pennines

ACCESS *Start from the village car park/WC on Luddenden Lane at southern approach. Halifax-Sowerby Bridge bus.*

From the car park turn right towards the village, keeping right on High Street as New Road climbs away. Before the bridge on Luddenden Brook bear left past new housing at Spring Bank, and a short path at the end leads to a stone-arched bridge. Across, a path runs upstream to emerge at High Street Fold. Go left over the bridge to the pub and church. *The charming village of Luddenden oozes with character: the attractive Lord Nelson sports a 1634 datestone, and Branwell Bronte drank here while ticket clerk at Luddenden Foot railway station. Across the tiny square a war memorial stands in front of St Mary's early 19th century church.*

From the war memorial double back left up above the pub to the foot of Old Lane on your right. *Alongside is the former St Mary's school (1856, extended 1928), with two corner doorways inscribed 'Midgley' and 'Warley' on the lintels, these being the two historic townships of Luddenden.* The setted lane climbs very steeply to a crossroads at the top. Turn right on Duke Street, becoming Rails Lane then Dean House Lane, a few minutes' stroll leading towards Oats Royd Mill. *Oats Royd House on the left was built in 1635 by James Murgatroyd, though the attractive frontage you see was added in the 19th century. The imposing Luddenden landmark of the Murgatroyd family's 19th century Oats Royd Mill with its tall chimney was in use up to the 1980s, but is now 21st century apartments.*

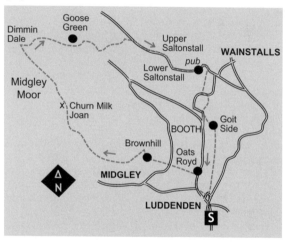

Immediately before Oats Royd House, turn left up the setted Delph Hill Lane. Past some houses it becomes grassier and ascends to a junction with a rough lane from the left: continue up to emerge onto another road, Thorney Lane. Go straight across to ascend the access road of Radcliffe Lane. At a house it swings right above it to rise, quickly ending at Brownhill Farm. Continue up the grassy way taking over beneath heathery moorland, quickly reaching a fence-stile onto the heather of Midgley Moor.

Turn left on a good path above the fence, with a wall soon taking over. *From here you look down on Luddenden Foot in the main valley, and increasingly more impressively to Cragg Vale, Broadhead Clough and Stoodley Pike.* The path leads delightfully on above a lone house until the fence/old wall ultimately drop away. Here the path bears gently right on a steady rise above old quarries to reach an outer wall corner, with the standing stone of Churn Milk Joan a minute higher at a path junction. *This sturdy six-footer may have been a medieval cross, and its hollowed top still sees the leaving of 'alms' for the needy.*

Leave by the clear path rising directly away (not the one by grouse butts to the right). This ascends gently through heather for some while. *At a level section look right to see Miller's Grave across to the right: this ancient burial site is most likely from the Bronze Age, and features a low, circular wall enclosing a boulder.* A little higher and the brow is reached, with slightly higher ground to your left and massive sweeps of moorland ahead. *Also well seen is the main valley driving a deep wedge beyond Hebden Bridge, with Stoodley Pike, Heptonstall and Old Town prominent.* Dropping down, the path is joined by one from the left as it quickly levels out. Ignore a lesser left fork in favour of tracing the distinct groove on your right by stone shooting butts in the depression known as Dimmin Dale.

Cross straight over a thin path here, and a minute further you reach a better path crossroads. Turn right on a good path dropping towards the Luddenden side of the moor. It curves right to pass the far end of the earlier shooting butts, then slants down to a fence/old wall at the well-defined moor edge. *Superb views into Luddenden Dean feature the Dean Head reservoirs near the valley head.* While a path runs along the edge to the right, instead pass through a gate in the fence to commence descent. Still on moor-like slopes, the path doubles back briefly towards the old wall. *Note the ruin of Castle Carr's old gatehouse in the trees up-dale. Castle Carr was a large Victorian castle amid ornamental gardens. Later abandoned, it fell into neglect and was finally dismantled in 1961. Down below, meanwhile, is the lower lodge.*

The path enjoys a well-graded slant down to the right, leaving the moor at a small gate just above Goose Green. A green way winds down between walls onto the enclosed track of Wood Lane by a house. Turn right on this for a couple of minutes then take a small gate on your left, descending a few stone steps into a field. Descend the wallside to a stile into trees above Luddenden Brook. Turn right on a thin path, and as the wall shortly starts to rise away, fork left to drop to stone-arched New Bridge on the brook.

Across, an enclosed path ascends left outside trees, rising to a stile. Here a briefly enclosed way slants right, opening out to a gate into a field. A faint way slants gently left across to a fence-stile ahead, then up again to a stile onto Heys Lane just short of Throstle Bower Farm. *Here is a burial ground attached to a Wesleyan Methodist Chapel destroyed by fire in 1954: note the old WC.*

Turn right along the traffic-free road, rising steadily before levelling out at Upper Saltonstall and continuing past Lower Saltonstall. *This super stroll on Saltonstall Lane offers immense views over the valley from these ancient hamlets: Lower Saltonstall was a vaccary (cattle farm) run by the Manor of Wakefield 700 years ago.* Shortly you arrive at the hidden Cat-i-the-Well pub. *Tucked away on a dead-end road, this enduring watering hole is a corruption of Caty Well, found on the roadside just above.* Immediately after the pub cross Catywell Bridge and as the road rises away, escape right on a driveway after the trees. This runs on to a house at Hock Cliff. Pass to its left via small gates to emerge into a broadening field. Take the thin path contouring away across the right side of the field, initially by a wall and then pleasantly along to emerge via a stile onto a road, Bank House Lane.

Rise a few paces left then double back right down setted Holme House Lane. Past a few houses it narrows to a footway running a superb course down the hillside, broadening back to an access road as it doubles back right past further houses to emerge back onto Bank House Lane. Drop left down to bridge Luddenden Brook, then turn left along an access road, Cow Lane. This runs along to the rows of houses at Goit Side. *One of these was a Friends' Meeting House of 1770.* Turn right to a cobbled fork at two characterful houses. *Here stood Dean Mills, with other mills once spread along here too.* Bear left, then keep straight on the broad track. This runs on to two final houses, from where the bridleway continues into trees. Very soon it emerges at another row of houses, Brook Terrace. At the end the access road goes left over the brook, but your way is straight on, and beyond some setts it narrows back to a bridleway. Its firm course in the company of Luddenden Brook runs to a fork just short of Luddenden village. Either takes you into the centre, the left one going via the church.

NORLAND MOOR

A colourful stroll around a popular pocket moorland

START *Norland (SE 065225; HX6 3RN)*

DISTANCE *6$\frac{1}{2}$ miles (10$\frac{1}{2}$km)*

ORDNANCE SURVEY 1:25,000 MAP
Explorer OL21 - South Pennines

ACCESS *Start from the crossroads of Shaw Lane, Clough Road and Berry Moor Road, by war memorial. Car park off Shaw Lane, along a short rough track by a play area on a corner of the moor. Bus from Halifax, Sowerby Bridge, Ripponden, West Vale.*

Scattered Norland 'Town' is an isolated hilltop settlement boasting splendid clothiers' houses of centuries past: some are revealed later. St Luke's church, a school and a fine old milestone are all centrally placed, while opposite the car park a three-storey house bears a 1743 datestone. Of greater relevance at the outset is Norland Moor, an island-like heather tract perched high above Sowerby Bridge and the Ryburn Valley. It bears the much-healed scars of extensive small-scale quarrying, notably along its western escarpment. From the car park take a broad path rising diagonally away to heathery old quarries on the brow. Forking within 50 strides, keep left to rise to a crossroads with a broader path. Turn right to rise very gently across the moor, passing above old quarry sites and along a gentle but obvious edge.

Beyond a covered reservoir where the Calderdale Way departs left, the more extensive quarries of Turgate Delph are passed, all totally reclaimed by the heather. *Just below on the roadside is the Moorcock Inn.* Forging on above the quarries, the main path bears left to the white-painted Ordnance Survey column at 931ft/284m. At the junction here turn right to regain the edge at the prominent Ladstone Rock. *This gritstone outcrop is a distinctive landmark with extensive views westwards over the Ryburn Valley featuring Crow Hill, Great Manshead Hill, Rishworth Moor, Blackstone Edge and the moors south of the M62.*

Resuming along the edge, the path soon drops towards the road. Without actually setting foot on tarmac, advance straight on a parallel path to the corner of the moor, with some chalets behind. Here take a clear path left to remain on the moor edge, rising by a wall. It soon gently veers away from it to a path junction at an

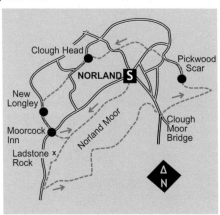

outer wall corner. Now bear right on the splendid wallside path, enjoying a very gentle decline through colourful vegetation. Reaching another corner, an enclosed way runs straight on, but you go left to again remain on the moor. Initially between walls, it then drops slightly to another outer corner. At this path crossroads go right to resume as before, on a broader path again gently declining with the boundary wall just to your right. Ignore a branch left and remain on the path near the moor edge, curving round to the left to absorb the Calderdale Way path at a solid cairn. *Ahead, the Wainhouse Tower can be discerned, completely dwarfing the mill chimneys and church spires. This famous landmark was built in the 1870s supposedly to serve a dyeworks, and is usually open for ascents on public holidays.*

Keep on to the wall corner near the edge of the moor. At this crossroads, under a pylon, turn right over a tiny stream to a road junction at Clough Moor Bridge. *An old boundary stone set into the bridge is inscribed 'Division of Norland and Elland'.* Cross the bridge, advance a few strides and take a wall-stile on the left to immediately re-enter colourful country. A thin path runs briefly left then turns downstream into quickly forming Maple Dean Clough, a riot of colourful vegetation. The way is steep and can demand caution when wet: at a fork remain on that nearest the stream. Further down the stream is crossed and quickly re-crossed, a little below which the bottom of the wood proper is reached. A fence deflects the path along through trees to the right, and when the fence turns away, the path drops a little to run on a level shelf into a break beneath overhead wires.

Here the path forks: while a branch rises right, your way slants down to the left into stately beeches to approach the rear of an isolated house. Just short of it take a thinner path doubling back left the short way down to meet a level path at a gateway at the foot of the wood. Go left on this largely flagged path along the base of the wood. The flags remain evident as the path passes through a small gate in an old wall and runs on to a footbridge over the clough. An intriguing, enclosed, setted path rises away, soon broadening into a track to reach a road end at the hamlet of Pickwood Scar. Head right on the road out, reaching a junction at a house. Here a flight of steps on the left sends a short, setted path up to a stile. The path climbs the field to another stile, then slants faintly up to a gate in the top right corner. A green lane runs the few strides right onto a road opposite Upper Old Hall. *Outstanding just down to the right is Lower Old Hall, with a 1634 datestone and a two-storey porch.*

Almost opposite is the former Blue Ball Inn, while visible just above it is Fallingworth Hall, dating from 1642 with mullioned windows and another two-storey porch. For a quick finish go to the junction above and turn right on Berry Moor Road. Cross straight over to the former pub car park, to a stile by a gate at the bottom corner. Contour across the field to a small metal gate in the wall ahead, and continue alongside an old vaccary wall. *A vaccary was a cattle farm. You now enjoy super views over Sowerby Bridge and up the valley.* At the end cross a walled green way and advance on, briefly enclosed, the route largely obvious as you pass through old stiles and along a field top. From a small gate at the end cross a field centre to a stile onto a road above Sowerby Croft.

Go briefly right to a kissing-gate opposite and a faint old way heads away along the field-top: Norland Moor appears above now. The increasingly flagged path soon swings right down to a small gate guarding a corner stile. Here an enclosed, flagged continuation curves round into an open area. Take the right fork, straight on into trees to emerge on Harper Royd Lane alongside a terrace at Clough Head. Go left on the footway along Hob Lane to rise past the Hobbit hotel. Ignore a right fork just after it and rise a little further towards a bend, where bear right on another flagged path. Emerging via a squeezer-stile into a field, the continuing fainter path keeps left with the wall. Maintain this direct line with partly flagged sections along two fieldsides to emerge via a stile/gate onto New Longley Lane above an old house at East Longley. Climb left past the intriguing terrace of New Longley to a T-junction at the Moorcock Inn. Cross to a parking area from where a former quarrymen's path slants left up onto the moor. Ignoring right branches, it passes between old quarries to meet the edge path of your outward route. Turn left to retrace opening steps.

The Ryburn Valley from Norland Moor

BLACK BROOK

A lively exploration of an unsung side valley

START *Stainland (SE 078195; HX4 9HF)*

DISTANCE *6^{3}4 miles (10^{3}4km)*

ORDNANCE SURVEY 1:25,000 MAP
Explorer OL21 - South Pennines

ACCESS *Start from the village centre. Memorial park car park on main street. Bus from Halifax, Elland and Huddersfield.*

The hilltop village of Stainland sits equidistant from Halifax and Huddersfield. St Andrew's church dates largely from 1840, with Stainland Cross stood opposite, while the massive former Providence Chapel of 1814 is now residential. Centrally placed is an imposing former Mechanics Institute of 1883, while the Duke of York is sole survivor of what well into the 21st century was a clutch of four pubs. Black Brook is a sizeable side valley of the Calder, beginning on Deanhead Moor and passing through Scammonden Reservoir to carve a deep course meeting the Calder below West Vale.

From the car park head east on the main street a short way and turn left on Drury Lane opposite the Duke of York, just a few strides after attractive Holroyd Square. *Beginning as a setted street, Drury Lane was made for carting stone from the quarries at its other end.* Beyond cottages it continues as a walled path between fields, at the end emerging onto a colourful brow above old quarries at Eaves Top. *This splendid viewpoint looks over the great sprawl of Halifax.* Advance a few paces to go left on the main track slanting down onto a grassy shelf beneath large quarried cliffs. Just yards short of an enormous free-standing boulder, a thin path doubles back right, rapidly becoming distinct to slant down a wooded bank between old walls. Within a minute it drops left to descend a colourful bank onto Halifax Bradley Hall golf course.

Go straight down over a fairway, passing right of a large clump of trees and down over a second fairway to the nearest trees below. A path drops down through them to escape the course at a hidden tee. Continue down a wooded bank, over a cross-path to a stile into a field. Drop slightly left to a stile at the bottom corner, emerging by a row of houses in the shadow of the derelict Gate

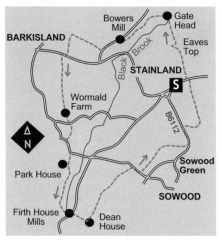

Head Mill. Advance briefly on the access road, and across the bridge turn upstream on an initially enclosed path shadowing Black Brook. Through several old pastures you approach the large Bowers Mill. In the last pasture you might be deflected slightly right by the stream diverted by a landslip. Rejoin the bank at a kissing-gate to approach the mill, bearing slightly right to a gate into the yard. Keep straight on between the buildings and up the access road at the end to join Branch Road. *This substantial mill now supports assorted business use, and features a cafe and attractive millpond.*

Go left on the footway until just past a bend: cross to a stile on the right immediately after a lone house, and after its garden wall ends a fenceside path slants right to the top corner of the field. From the stile head straight up the side of tree-lined Sandyfoot Clough, soon leaving the trees but clinging to the clough side. This grand climb ends when there seems no obvious way ahead. From a stile in the adjacent fence, rise by a crumbling wall to a wall corner above. Pass a red-brick shed to a stile/gate onto a walled grass track, and at the end take a small gate by a larger one ahead into the grounds of Barkisland Hall. *This gem from 1638 boasts a magnificent three-storey front.* The enclosed path runs parallel with its short drive to a gate out onto Stainland Road at the foot of Barkisland. Turn up the main street of this characterful village: your point of departure is a narrow stile on the left alongside the village stocks. *Just a little further up the street are the rather splendid Nolson House and then the Griffin Inn, both on the right.*

Departing, a short snicket leaves the stile to enter a field. An enclosed grassy path descends to Barkisland Clough, crossing a slab bridge and bearing left up the bank to a stile preceding stone steps out of the trees. *Good open views look down over the valley to the left, and back over Barkisland.* Rise away with an old wall and along to a stile onto the cart track of Howroyd Lane. From a gate/stile opposite, follow a wall away: over a streamlet slab at a line of trees resume with a wall rising to a corner stile at the top. Now bear left across the field to a corner gate into the yard at Wormald: on your left is a modern barn conversion. *Pause to admire the beautiful old house on your right with its mullioned and transomed windows and a 1694 datestone on the porch.* Don't follow the drive out but take a stile on the left opposite the house, and cross the field to the wooded top of Bottomley Clough.

A stile admits onto a road, Bottomley Lane: go left a few strides then take a stile on the right. Head away with the wall to a corner stile, then cross to a stile ahead. Maintain this straight line along the bottom of several narrow fields linked by old stiles beneath Steel Lane Head. At the end a wall returns in a longer field to lead on to a corner stile and old wall-stile: a short drive beneath houses leads out onto Steel Lane. Go left, down just as far as a sharp, setted bend. Here bear right on a drive towards Park House Farm. When it swings up to the house, continue along the cart track ahead, soon ending at a gate into a field. Don't pass through but take the contrastingly enclosed path descending left. Several twists and turns see it run to the right above woodland. Ignore a thinner path ahead at a fork, and remain on the broad continuation slanting left down through trees to meet Black Brook at a weir.

A brief stroll upstream leads to a bridle-gate/stile, and a small footbridge on the brook. Across, a path runs between modern housing at Firth House Mills onto their access road. Rising gently away to the left, leave before reaching a house on the gentle brow ahead. From an easily missed stile on the right, squeeze up a few stone steps into a field corner and ascend the fieldside to a stile in the next corner. Rise away with a fence, and as its swings right, follow it up to beneath solitary Dean House. Ignore the small metal gate and rise left outside its confining wall, reaching another such gate alongside the house. Go left the short way up the drive to a crossroads of access roads.

Go straight across onto Dean House Lane, rising gently then levelling out above New Manor House. This rough lane now runs a level course all the way along to join Forest Hill Road. *Initially beneath colourful slopes and former quarries, this promenade offers big views over the valley, including much of the earlier route: further along at Mount Pleasant Farm, Stainland appears not far ahead.* Turn right up the road, passing a few houses on the edge of Sowood. Just before a steeper section you reach lanes going off either way: take the left option of Moor Hey Lane, resuming much as your previous one. Beyond Only House of 1884, at Shaw Cottage it becomes a nicer cart track. Passing modern housing you reach a fork in front of a short terrace, on the edge of Sowood at Sowood Green. Keep to the left branch, descending to emerge onto the B6112. *To your right is an old milestone and a former school.*

Go left on the footway, quickly reaching the edge of Stainland. *Simplest option is to remain on this to be finished within minutes.* For a varied finish, take a signed path right at the speed limit just before a row of houses on the right. A walled cart track heads pleasantly away, encountering a short kink where it transforms into a footpath swinging left. A few steps further, leave by a wall-stile set back on the left, and head away with the wall on your left. Through several fields linked by old wall-stiles, a brow reveals Stainland surrounding its church just below. Down to the right is the side valley of Holywell Brook. Descend the rough grass with the wall to a corner stile. More rough grass sees you rise away, now with a wall on the right, passing odd caravans to ascend a short access road back onto the village street. The start point is just to the left.

NORTH DEAN WOOD

Beautiful woodland leads to a lengthy towpath trod

START *West Vale (SE 096213; HX4 8AN)*

DISTANCE *5^{3}4 miles (9^{1}4km)*

ORDNANCE SURVEY 1:25,000 MAP
Explorer OL21 - South Pennines

ACCESS *Start from Brig Royd car park at junction of B6112 and B6113 at West Vale crossroads, Brow Bridge. Bus from Halifax, Huddersfield and Elland.*

West Vale is based around a busy crossroads on the edge of contiguous Greetland. Victoria Mills, North Dean Mill and several shops and pubs are close by, with a cafe at the very start. From the rear of the car park a footbridge on Black Brook puts you into Clayhouse Park. Bear right towards Clay House, part hidden by trees. A path drops to a lower grassy area, and on your left stone steps ascend through gardens to arrive in front of the house itself. *This is a most impressive yeoman clothier's house with a fine facade of mullioned and transomed windows. Dating from the 17th century, it is now managed by the local authority. Alongside is an aisled barn with a magnificent low-slung roof: it was restored in 1986 and converted into private dwellings. An array of old local boundary stones is embedded in the wall on the access road to your left.*

Pass between the house and the old barn, and a few steps to the left take you up a grassy area to a broad track behind a wall gap on the edge of woodland. Turn left just a couple of paces, and bear right off the broad track to a wall-stile just ahead. This sends a path rising through trees. *The hollow here is the course of the short Stainland branch line. It opened in 1875 and closed in the 1950s, and West Vale station stood on the far side of the B6112, by a surviving viaduct.* Rising with a tall fence on your left, when this quickly ends take the level path left, soon emerging at the head of a rough access track. In the corner ahead an enclosed setted path ascends onto an access track. Go left, quickly becoming a grassy cart track as it runs on above four stone terraces. At the last of these, take a path on the right into trees. Crossing a track it climbs steeply to emerge onto a minor road in front of a house.

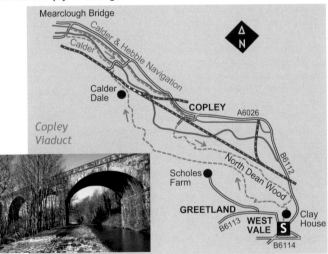

Go right the short way to a junction, and double back left on an access road between houses. This quickly reaches a junction, where go right. This walled track of Collin Lane heads away between fields, improving to a grassy cart track to approach North Dean Wood. The final short section is a narrow footway into the wood top. Go left to commence a splendid, sustained wood top ramble, with very steep woods and craggy bluffs below and fields to the left. *Snatched views to the valley feature the massive Copley Viaduct, with the Wainhouse Tower high above. This famous landmark was built in the 1870s to serve a dyeworks.* Rising very gradually, and ignoring all branches, this grand stride eventually emerges onto a rough road. Just half a minute along to the right is a junction where the road slants down into the trees, a driveway goes left, and the Calderdale Way resumes along the wood top.

Ignore all these in favour of the right-most option, a clear path dropping right of the road. It runs a splendid sunken course down the wood, passing above the lone cottage of Lower Tinker Hey with views of viaduct and river. At its far wall corner a stone flight sends a short-cut path down onto rough North Dean Road. Leaving the woodland here gives big views over the valley. Take a stile straight across onto a wide enclosed way. From a stile just ahead, a thin path crosses the narrow field bottom to another stile. Just yards further take one on your left, and a wallside path resumes to drop gently to a corner stile onto an old walled footway. Turn down this to emerge into a field at the bottom. Go briefly left on a faint embanked way, then drop right on a thin path to a footbridge on Maple Dean Clough. Cross to a stile in front to join an access road. Go right, swinging left at an attractive pond by a house. *This was the location of the enigmatically named Calder Dale Grease Works.*

The road runs alongside a railway embankment to shortly pass under the long, high railway arch at Hollas Bridge. It then runs left to join an access road by an industrial estate. Go right a few steps then take a path on the left before the modern bridge to join the River Calder. A firm path runs a pleasant course upstream amid greenery with the new housing of Calder View opposite, before emerging at another industrial area at double-arched Mearclough Bridge. Cross the road bridge and leave immediately by dropping onto the canal towpath. Turn right to commence the return with the Calder & Hebble Navigation. *This opened in 1770 to link the River Calder with the Rochdale Canal at Sowerby Bridge.*

Soon you pass the modern housing of Calder View at Edward Road Bridge at the former Canal Mills. Beyond Stern Mill Bridge you enjoy a sustained, splendid leafy section until passing beneath an arch of Copley Viaduct. *This mighty 23-arch bridge of 1852 spans the valley on the Halifax-Burnley/Rochdale line.* After further modern housing you approach Copley canal bridge. *Just over it on the main road is the Volunteers Arms.* Use a gap to join Copley Lane, and double back right down it to pass under a railway into Copley. *The attractive houses on your right are part of mill-owner Edward Akroyd's 1840s model village: the mill was demolished in 1974.* As it bends right alongside a rugby club, bear left to Copley Bridge back over the river. *Erected in 2017 it replaced the original toll bridge of 1831 which was destroyed by floods in December 2015. On the far bank are an enormous church and an old toll-house. The redundant St Stephen's church of 1865 closed in 1993 and is now in the care of the Churches Conservation Trust, often open to visitors. The octagonal tollhouse of Copley Bridge Bar dates from the 1830s, and features a restored notice of tolls.*

Advance on the rough North Dean Road (again) just a few paces to where it turns right to ascend North Dean Wood again. Here take a gap-stile on the left and follow a level path above the church. Immediately forking, take the gently ascending right branch. When this also quickly forks, remain on the level left option beneath tall, stately beeches. With steep slopes above, this rises only slightly to quickly arrive at the edge of a murky pool. Across its minimal outflow ascend wooden steps to a path junction, then rise right up further steps to a guidepost sending you back right up to another junction on a bouldery knoll. *This grand spot looks down on the pool.* Go left to commence a near-level stride for a considerable time, trading the beeches for myriad oaks above a bracken carpet. The outward route is just a stone's throw above.

Further on, a more open section runs through bracken before re-entering trees at the end. *Below you is the site of Greetland station.* The path runs above a boundary wall, rising marginally through colourful surrounds as a broad path merges from the right: up above are further crags. A little further comes a fork on a brow beneath a sizeable crag: as the broader left option drops gently away, remain on the thinner but very clear level path ahead. Merging into a broader track rising from the left, this surmounts a minor brow and passes through an old quarry site to a gate behind a house. Just beyond, you join its access track to find yourself back on the outward route. Descend the enclosed setted footway on your left and simply drop down the rough road below to cross onto the grass alongside Clay House.

SHIBDEN DALE

A charming valley explored from a historic old house

START *Shibden Park (SE 108260; HX3 6XG)*

DISTANCE *5³⁄4 miles (9¹⁄4km)*

ORDNANCE SURVEY 1:25,000 MAP
Explorer 288 - Bradford & Huddersfield

ACCESS *Start from Mereside car park off A58 Godley Lane, a short mile east of Halifax town centre. Bus from Halifax.*

Shibden Hall is focal point of the hugely popular Shibden Park on the edge of Halifax. From its lofty perch overlooking the park it dates back to 1420, and has seen various additions down the years, highlight being its half-timbered Tudor front. It spent three centuries in the hands of the mill-owning Lister family, most famous being 19th century diarist Anne. Acquired as a museum by Halifax Corporation in 1933, its adjoining 17th century aisled barn and restored workshops feature a horse-drawn carriage collection and displays relating to numerous rural crafts. Attractions of the park and gardens include a cafe, miniature railway, boating lake, pitch & putt course and a drystone walling exhibition.

At the far end of the main car park behind the café, a gate accesses a bridge over Shibden Brook. Advance along cul-de-sac Red Beck Road, and at the junction ahead take a gap opposite, from where a short path climbs through trees onto the A58 at

Stump Cross. Cross with care to a gap opposite, and a setted path slants left into trees. It then runs an enclosed course into the charming hamlet of Shibden Fold. Keep straight on between the buildings, and along an enclosed access track to the last house, Longfield Farm. Also look right to a grand old house across the meadow. Keep straight on a flagged path the short way to a slab stile onto a flagged path junction. From the bridle-gate in front slant left up a pair of fields to a top corner stile. It now runs right, part flagged between trees and fields to emerge onto an access track. Go right on this until just before Hall Houses. Leave by a stile on the left and ascend a wallside to a corner stile into more open country.

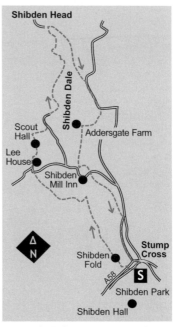

A thin path rises left onto a little brow, soon meeting another path to turn right on this broad ridge. At a knoll just ahead, it swings left at the edge of the trees to slant right up a colourful bank. Meeting another little path coming in from the left, keep right. Through a few trees it runs back into open country, again on a small spur with a slight hollow to your left. Just before the end of this open spur it bears left again in scattered trees, rising to the end of the trees and a small clearing, with a path coming down from the left. Advance straight on, dropping slightly to almost at once face another fork. Your main one goes left to join an old wall, and follows it right the few yards before the wall expires. The path runs straight on across another open bank, through a scant wall and on beneath an outer wall corner where it slants gently down across extensive bilberry slopes. Stiles at the end lead through a sliver of trees, from where the lower path across one final enclosure leads on above a wall outside a house to a stile onto the setted Lee Lane.

Go briefly left to the hairpin bend above, and go right on a rough access road past Lee House on the right. *It was designed by the celebrated John Carr of York in 1766 for the Stocks family, local mine-owners and brewers.* The road drops steadily down to arrive dramatically in front of Scout Hall. *Completed in 1681 for silk merchant John Mitchell, this imposing 'calendar building' of 12 bays, with 52 doors and (supposedly) 365 panes of glass has been derelict since the 1980s.* Pass to its right and a rougher track continues through a gate/stile into a small rough enclosure. From a fence-stile by the wall corner on the right, an enclosed, part-flagged path descends a fieldside, steepening at the bottom to reach a slab footbridge high above Shibden Brook, a nice corner. Steps zigzag up the other side to quickly emerge onto a minor road, Sim Carr Lane.

Go left, swinging uphill to end at attractive Lower Lime House. Don't take the drive behind it to Upper Lime House, but continue straight up the broad track to a T-junction of such ways just above. Turn left on the main way, running above that final house and on a splendid level path as Bare Head Lane. Reaching a fork in deeper trees, go left on a level path running a delightful course beneath a steep bilberry bank. Entering woodland it drops beneath beeches to soon reach a footbridge on Shibden Brook in a shady dell.

Across, the path slants up then quickly doubles back left to the wood top at an old gateway. Take the path rising right out into a large, flat clearing. Cross it to the left where two paths rise into a wooded bank, quickly merging to climb left out of the wood. This rapidly becomes an enclosed old way climbing to meet a firm access road. Turn right on this, rising steadily above the woodland to pass through a gate. With housing on the edge of Shibden Head above, take the right branch a few strides to reach an intriguing installation. *The crane here is on the century-old site of both a quarry and a colliery.* Though an inviting path heads straight on, your way is the path sharp right beneath a tall wall into trees. Ignoring any left branches this drops down on a steep bank high above the stream, a super descent to reach a confluence with a stream from the left. Just a couple of paces left this sidestream is crossed by stepping-stones.

The onward path is easily missed, but slants right up the wooded bank, with a steep drop to the main beck to your right. It then runs a delightful contour above the drop to meet another sidestream's deep groove. The path swings left here up into open country, rising a little to run to the head of that streamlet. In front of it is a fork, with the slim left branch rising through open country. On fading, it's only a stone's throw to a path along the bank top. Turn right to the massive wall ahead, rejoining Bare Head Lane in front of it. *This remarkable structure is at the site of one of numerous small collieries in the area.* Make use of a fascinating feature by passing through the doorway in it, and a flagged tunnel runs through to emerge into a field alongside upright flagstones. Continue away with the wall to a stile ahead, then left along the field edge the short way to a stile/gate onto a road, Green Lane.

Go right for a few minutes to drop to a sharp bend. *En route on the left is Lower North Royd, a lovely old house dated 1699.* At the bend go right on unsurfaced Addersgate Lane, dropping gently to the eponymous farm. Immediately before it take a slim gateway on the left to descend the hedgeside, dropping to a stile. Maintain this course down the centre of a meadow and a couple of fieldsides to an equestrian yard at Dam Head. Continue down to emerge on the drive leading out left. This quickly drops onto a narrow lane. *Quickest way to Shibden Mill Inn is to go right then quickly left.* Rise very briefly left to turn right along an enclosed twin-flagged track, The Dicken, which runs pleasantly along to another road. *The very attractive and immensely popular pub is just one minute down to the right at a historic mill site, with the car park on the old millpond.*

From a stile/gate opposite, a grassy track crosses a sloping pasture, maintaining this course through a further field to meet a wall and acquire a twin-flagged surface. *A worn groove indicates historic use by carts.* This leads on to a gate by a house, whose short drive runs to a road. Without setting foot on it, take the inviting setted Staups Lane to the right, slanting down to become surfaced at the bottom and along to the A58 again at Stump Cross. *The Stump Cross Inn is to your left, with a former tollbooth just past it.* Cross with care and go left a few strides to branch right down Old Godley Lane. This quickly doubles back to meet your outward route, returning down Red Beck Road to the start.

OVENDEN MOOR

Richly varied upland walking from a popular reservoir

START *Ogden (SE 066308; HX2 8XZ)*

DISTANCE *5¹⁄4 miles (8¹⁄2km)*

ORDNANCE SURVEY 1:25,000 MAP
Explorer OL21 - South Pennines

ACCESS *Start from water company car park at Ogden Water, on Ogden Lane off A629 at Causeway Foot pub. Bus from Halifax.*

Built in 1858, Ogden Water offers woodland paths and an easy reservoir circuit. There is a visitor centre with refreshments and WCs between car park and dam. At the end of the lower car park a kissing-gate sends a broad path into the trees. Absorbing another, it angles gently towards the reservoir, meeting a lower, level path just short of the end. Near the head of the reservoir you reach a footbridge over a tiny side dam. While the reservoir circuit path crosses it, your way goes straight on, a thinner path that within a minute meets a broader one coming in from the right. Bear left on this, and ignoring an early left fork downhill, forge pleasantly on, rising gently before dropping down to run tightly with the lively beck.

The end of the wood is quickly reached, and a stile sends a path on through the open country of Ogden Clough. Remain on your bank as two footbridges offer an alternative south bank section. This steep-walled clough is a little gem, and the beckside path soon reaches twin waterfalls where the peaty moorland stream tumbles over gritstone ledges. At the second falls the path rises to a junction alongside a sturdy bridge over a little dam: immediately upstream are gritstone crags. Across the waterworks bridge a path rises away to a stile onto the broad heather sweep of Ovenden Moor, with its wind turbines looming just ahead. Shadowed by a fence to the left, a broad path heads away towards them, rising imperceptibly to a brow. The wind turbines are now almost within touching distance, while just ahead the former Withens Hotel and two masts appear.

The path drops to a bridge in Skirden Clough, then rises as a broader track to a kissing-gate onto the firm track of Withens New Road. Turn right to a kissing-gate onto Cold Edge Road at The Withens. *Into the 21st century this was the Withens Hotel, built in 1862 to serve quarrymen, and until its closure the highest pub in* 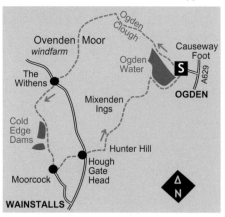 *West Yorkshire. Behind it, the unmissable Ovenden Moor windfarm has been operational since 1993: its 23 100ft high turbines were replaced by 9 more efficient 270ft ones in 2016.*

To resume, go a few strides left and turn right down a walled cart track. This swings left then down to the right to ruinous farm buildings. Passing to their right it runs between old walls along to the restored Haighcote Barn. Again passing right, its access road is joined to swing left to approach the Cold Edge Dams. Just short of the first one, Haigh Cote Dam, branch off to join a thin path along the embankment. *This is the home of Halifax Water Ski Club.* Follow this to the far end of the main embankment. The path then crosses a little tract of heather moorland to do likewise on the smaller Leadbeater Dam. At the first corner, however, turn down a grassy path across further moorland towards a clump of trees, passing to their right. Instead of going left to a gate, a thinner path goes straight ahead to locate a corner stile below, admitting onto the rough road left earlier. Go right for two minutes to the first buildings, absorbing the Calderdale Way for the next half-mile.

Immediately after the buildings on the left turn into the yard at Moorcock Farm. *The main building is now unrecognisable as the isolated Moorcock pub this was until as recently as 2002.* Past the right of the house take a small gate into a moist, reedy pasture, following a fence along to a stile ahead. A narrow, enclosed path heads away beneath cattle sheds and a small dam, then along a flagged fieldside onto another walled rough road opposite some houses. Go left a few strides, then from a stile on the right cross straight over the field to a plank footbridge. Ascend the wallside behind, and part way up cross a stile to resume up the other side of a fence. Over a stile at the top the path goes round to the left of Hough Gate Head, and up a track to join its drive just before rejoining Cold Edge Road.

Once again go left a few strides, then from a kissing-gate on the right a grassy track heads away. After a spell between walls it swings gently right, descending steadily into a quarried area at Hunter Hill. The Calderdale Way heads into the heart of this varied scene, but you must part company. At a crossroads of tracks the Way prepares to become enclosed again: here take the inviting branch left towards four sycamores. *The low ruins in their shadow are all that remains of Hunter Hill Farm: the area here is known as Slaughter Gap, named after a 1644 Civil War skirmish.*

After the last ruin a thin trod contours across to a kissing-gate at a wall junction onto a grassy corner of Ovenden Moor. Follow the wall away until it turns off, then a fence shadows the thin path to the edge of steeper slopes above a colourful hollow occupied by a golf course. The thin path descends to a stile onto the course: cross a fairway then bear gently left on a grass track, over a cross-paths to a substantial bridge on the central stream. A short way further, alongside a green, a thin path scales the slope alongside a patch of bracken, soon slanting right and broadening as you gain height along the bracken fringe. On the brow, shortly turn left to head straight across another two fairway paths to rejoin Withens New Road in front of the reservoir plantation. Turn right on this to quickly drop down to the dam, which is crossed to finish.

MAG DALE

Delectable woodland is at the heart of this lovely valley

START *Armitage Bridge (SE 134136; HD4 7PD)*

DISTANCE *6 miles (9½km)*

ORDNANCE SURVEY 1:25,000 MAP
Explorer 288 - Bradford & Huddersfield

ACCESS *Start from the B6110 Armitage Road between church and mill off A616. Huddersfield-Holmfirth bus. Berry Brow station nearby.*

Armitage Bridge is a village on the River Holme, dominated by the massive Brooke's Mill. This former woollen mill with its fine chimney dates from 1798, and now supports modern businesses as well as a cafe. St Paul's church of 1848 was restored after a 1987 fire. Facing the church turn right along the road, then quickly right up Bankfoot Lane. As it starts to climb more, take an enclosed path on the left after a white house. This rises gently between walls and into trees, a super way slanting gently up a wooded bank. Keep straight on through more open woodland, and at a fork, take the right branch with old walls again to emerge onto Hawkroyd Bank Road.

Go left between open fields, soon reaching a T-junction: go left and remain on this road as it turns sharply right as White Gate down into Mag Dale. Soon arriving at Magdale Bridge on Mag Brook, don't cross but go right beneath the short row of cottages. A broad path enters a corner of Spring Wood to head off through Mag Dale.

69

Rising away, within a few strides take a left branch through an old stile. This sends a good little path along the wood bottom, almost at once passing an exuberant streamlet emerging from craggy Spring Head Well. The path continues through springtime bluebells and hollies, and a broader way slants in from the right. Drawing level with derelict Lord's Mill over to the left in the valley bottom, a junction is reached. Take the path slanting right, quickly joined by an earlier branch just before the junction. A long steady slant through the wood brings arrival at a gate into the yard of a house at Wood End: continue up its access road rising away. *This offers super views over the valley, a scrubby bank falling to Cocking Steps Mill below, while Meltham Moor fills the skyline above its town.*

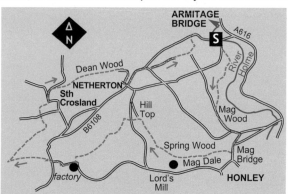

Reaching a cluster of houses at Hill Top, advance just a few strides further and take a signed path before the first house on the left. Its enclosed course drops pleasantly down to the rear of some cottages onto Lea Lane. Cross to a small gate and a continuing path drops down steps, quickly swinging left between old walls to emerge into a field. Drop slightly left to a footbridge in the hedge below, and head away through the field centre on the flat valley floor. Passing through a bridle-gate and on again to a stile, advance again to pass outside the grounds of a house on the left. Just beyond is a tiny slab streamlet and a kissing-gate by further houses. Turn right on the access road, running out past new houses onto a road at a factory. Turn right, with a short pull through a dismantled rail bridge. *This was on the short branch line to Meltham from the Huddersfield-Sheffield line at Lockwood, opened in 1868 and fully closed in 1965.* Just before the road above, a little path cuts left up steps onto the B6108.

Go right a few yards and cross at the bus shelter to a stile/gate opposite. An enclosed path ascends a fieldside to a stile into Bank Wood, rising gently to meet a rough cross-track at the top. Go straight over up a short path to a stile out of the wood. A thin path continues gently up through two field centres to a stile onto the head of a track, Far Fields Lane. Double back right on this, running a walled course between fields to a T-junction. Go left the short way to emerge on Whitehead Lane, crossing straight over to the nicer grassy way of Turbid Lane. This is quickly left by a still nicer walled footway to the right, running a pleasant course out onto a road at South Crosland. *On your left is a fine set of stone troughs at Crab Tree Well, alongside a pinfold for impounding stray animals.*

Cross the road and turn down Sandy Lane opposite, into trees, quickly leaving by a path right into Dean Wood before bridging a stream. This path runs a magical course through the wood: the stream drops steeply away into the deep Dean Clough but your path undulates along under the wood top amid bluebells. Just past an old quarry it forks: bear right on the main path the short way to a cross-paths. Take the left branch, rapidly absorbing the earlier left fork and running on to suddenly emerge onto the head of suburban Deyne Road on the edge of Netherton. Advance on this, still with woodland on your left. At the bottom it swings right to a junction at a Methodist church. Drop left down Chapel Street the short way to the B6108 through Netherton.

Turn left on the footway, and after a few minutes bear right up narrow Delph Lane. Quickly leave this by cul-de-sac Bourn View Road on the left. This runs a dead-straight course, always with housing on the right, to meet a traffic impasse. Keep on amid woodland to meet suburbia again as the road swings sharp right. Here advance straight on a cart track through a gate into Old Spring Wood. Quickly absorbing a bridleway from the right, drop left on the hard track to a sharp left bend just below. With paths going right and straight ahead, take the latter, a super path dropping down to some houses at Wood End, becoming surfaced to drop down onto the B6110. Turn right the short way back to the start.

CASTLE HILL

An outstanding Iron Age fort high above the Holme Valley

START *Honley (SE 138119; HD9 6AA)*

DISTANCE *6^{1}4 miles (10km)*

ORDNANCE SURVEY 1:25,000 MAP
Explorer 288 - Bradford & Huddersfield

ACCESS *Start from the village centre. Car park on
Westgate. Huddersfield-Holmfirth bus. Railway station.*

Honley is an independent Holme Valley village, with St Mary's
*church of 1843 amid old buildings on the attractive setted Church
Street. Old stocks can be found in the churchyard. Honley Show
takes place in June.* From the centre turn down Eastgate, swinging
right at the bottom to a crossroads with the A6024 Woodhead Road.
Cross and go along short-lived Station Road to the junction with the
A616. Turn right, cross at the island just a little further, then left
on Gynn Lane. Almost at once branch right on Marsh Platt Lane, an
access road that rises to end at two driveways. Immediately after
the left one a path goes left to a stile into a field corner. A thin
path ascends the left side to a stile at the top, and a bridle-gate
just behind accesses a rail underpass. Turn right to a corner gate,
and ignoring the continuing path, take a stile on the left. Ascend
the field to a fence corner, then up with the fence to a fine pair of
stiles at the top corner. *Look back over Honley to Meltham Moor.*

From the left stile an enclosed path runs towards the large house of Hollinhurst, and a stile puts you on its drive to go right on the access road out to Hall Ing Lane. Virtually opposite, a cart track heads away into West Wood. Immediately after a field on the right ends you meet a cross-paths. Turn right up this, a splendid slant up through the bluebell wood, then left along the top to emerge above a scrubby bank. The path soon arrives at a fork, where keep left along the bank top. Towards the end an old stile sees you into the trees of Sawgates Clough, a good path tracing the wood top to cross the streamlet. The path then ascends steps to a gap into a field corner. Rise away with an old wall on your left, the path soon easing out. Maintain this same course past Glen Farm and along to a stile onto Honley Road. *Castle Hill is now well seen over to the left.* Cross to the footway and rise the short way into Farnley Tyas.

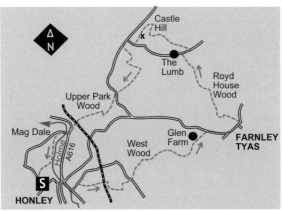

The hilltop village of Farnley Tyas looks across the tranquil Woodsome Valley to Castle Hill. At its heart are the church of St Lucius, and the Golden Cock. Keep on past the pub, going left at the junction. Within a few strides turn down the enclosed cart track of Cliffe Lane, after the first house. This drops away and swings sharp left to end at a bench. *This serene viewpoint for the upper section of this ramble is appropriately inscribed 'Majestic Castle stands proudly among the hills'.* Through the kissing-gate turn right down the fieldside to a gate/stile part way down. A broad path descends

Royd House Wood, crossing a small stream and on to briefly emerge from trees. Almost immediately re-entering woods, it runs a short, level course to leave the trees at the other side. Pass right of the boundary wall heading away, a path shadowing its continuing hedge down to a stile at the end. A path heads away through the scattered trees of Molly Carr Wood, descending steps to Lumb Dike.

A bridge crosses the stream and the path ascends the other side to a gate. Ascend the field with a fence on your left, and up a second fieldside to a stile at the top at The Lumb. Turn briefly right on Lumb Lane to a stile on the left for a steep fieldside climb to a stile at the top. Resume uphill to a stile onto a firm access road. Just to your left another stile maintains the climb, becoming enclosed in greenery to slant left into colourful undergrowth. At the rear of a near-hidden house a signed path doubles back right, out of the undergrowth to emerge alongside a fence with open views. Immediately above you is the outer bank of Castle Hill fort. Follow the path right with the fence onto the end of the site, where rise to meet a firm path encircling the outer bank. Go right on this back round the other side of the fort, or at a cross-paths, ascend to follow the bank top. Either way will take you to the Victoria Tower.

Castle Hill looms high above its surroundings, its noble stature further enhanced by the imposing tower commemorating Queen Victoria's Diamond Jubilee of 1897. It is normally open afternoons at holidays and weekends, and for a fee you can climb to survey the massive panorama. Most impressive scene is westwards, where Meltham Moor fronts many miles of Pennine moorland. Castle Hill is best known for the Iron Age hillfort that existed here in a ready-made location. The extensive ditches and ramparts were later incorporated into the defences of a motte and bailey castle around 800 years ago by the de Lacys: a well and modest sections of wall survive. The castle became a hunting lodge before falling into ruin around 1320. This beacon site was used to warn of the approach of the Spanish Armada in 1588, and a modern day beacon celebrates noteworthy occasions. Political, religious and social rallies took place here notably in the 19th century, along with what would today be deemed unsavoury 'sporting' events. A World War Two anti-aircraft battery was also placed here. The Castle Hill Hotel first built here in 1810 was replaced in 1852: demolished in 2005 after planning violations, replacement plans are in a state of limbo.

Leave by a hard path running a few strides from the tower to a long flight of steps down onto a road. Go right to a T-junction, then left. At the second house on the left take a stile set back across its yard, and follow a wall away. At a kink in it go sharp right across the field centre to an outer corner, and through a gateway turn left to resume along the wall. Through an intervening stile this leads to a gateway in the bottom wall. Through it turn sharp right to a gate/stile above Roaf Wood, and on again through a corner stile ahead, leaving the wood edge to rise with a wall on your left. At a bend part way up pass through the stile and a thin path turns right with the wall, rising then running on to emerge onto Hey Lane.

Cross and go right a few strides to a gate/stile, and take the path heading away with a hedge on the right. At the end it drops to a fence-stile, and forks. Take the right one dropping to a stile into Yorkshire Wildlife Trust's Upper Park Wood. A good path drops directly away through the trees, quickly emerging at a kissing-gate onto the top of a nice grassy bank. Go right the short way to a stile/gate back into the wood. Advance briefly to a dip, then take a thinner path down the near side of a streamlet. This descends nicely, over a cross-paths and down past a tiny pond to quickly emerge via a stile into a small clearing. Just ahead the path runs to a kissing-gate into the wood edge. The path resumes down the side, emerging at the bottom in front of a rail underpass. *This proves an eerie experience, being dark, quite narrow and very long.* At the other end you emerge overlooking the A616.

Go left a few strides on the side road to join the main road at a filling station, and cross via an island. Go briefly left and turn right, unpromisingly along a business park road. After bridging the River Holme, turn sharp left on an access road tracing a mill-cut to a short row of houses. Beyond them a firm path takes over alongside the cut, quickly reaching its start at a weir. Forking a little further beneath an easily missed millpond, take the left branch to a foot-bridge on Mag Brook just ahead. The firm path emerges into a field, and heads away above the Holme. Through the two pastures of Magdale Fields it meets an access road-end at a path junction. Take the walled, setted path rising to the right, swinging left to emerge onto an access road at modern houses. Rise briefly up, then bear left on St Mary's Road. This swings right after the church to emerge onto Church Street, with the starting point just down to the left.

HOLME VALLEY

Appreciable ups and downs in this delightful adventure

START *Holmfirth (SE 141081; HD9 1HA)*

DISTANCE *5$\frac{1}{2}$ miles (8$\frac{3}{4}$km)*

ORDNANCE SURVEY 1:25,000 MAP
Explorer OL1 - Peak District, Dark Peak or
Explorer 288 - Bradford & Huddersfield

ACCESS *Start from the town centre. Car parks. Bus from*
Huddersfield, Slaithwaite, Meltham, Wakefield, Sheffield.

    Holmfirth is the hub of the Holme Valley, a characterful place
of nooks and crannies. Holy Trinity church replaced one damaged
in a flood of 1777, but a far worse disaster was the Bilberry Dam
flood of 1852, in which 81 lives were lost along with mills, houses and
bridges. For decades Holmfirth was best known for saucy seaside
postcards first produced by Bamforth & Co. Less well known is their
pioneer work with silent films long before Hollywood became the
place to be. The town boasted a postcard museum in the latter
part of the 20th century. From 1973 to 2010 it was the antics of a
trio of juvenile pensioners in TV's Last of the Summer Wine that
put Holmfirth on the map. Until 1959 a branch line ran just two
miles from Brockholes on the Penistone line. An old tollhouse is
centrally placed, and a fine old milestone is set into the bridge.
An old cinema has been transformed into a popular concert venue.

From the junction of Victoria Street with the main road in the town centre, go left a few strides on Huddersfield Road, and just before the Library/Information Centre, take a path climbing into the sloping Victoria Park. Remain on the main setted path which curves up to the right, crossing a broad level path. From the top corner a snicket runs out onto a road, Cooper Lane. Turn up this to a T-junction with Binns Lane just ahead. Go right a few yards and turn up a path squeezing between gardens. It climbs very steeply through trees to run out between drives onto an access road at Hill. Go left, leaving the houses for a rapid move into countryside. The rough road of Hill Lane continues as a walled track between the fields. *Over to the right are the first views down the valley to the prominent tower on Castle Hill above Huddersfield.* The track runs unfailingly on to rise into Upperthong at a sharp bend in the road.

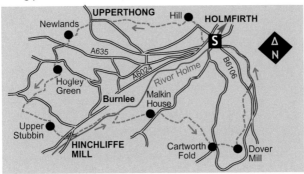

The hilltop village of Upperthong is an old weaving settlement, and a prominent reminder is the three-storeyed Weavers House on the main street. Upperthong is home to the World Welly Wanging Championship, which takes place on the village's gala weekend. For the uninitiated, to 'wang' something is to throw it! Head straight along Towngate, passing the Royal Oak to a junction with Wickens Lane at the far end. Bear left down Broad Lane, down through another sharp bend out of the village. *This brings spacious views as the upper Holme Valley opens out, dominated by the mass of Black Hill with Holme Moss TV mast prominent.* Within yards take a stile on the right, and cross the field centre to the next one. From this, turn down the wallside to a stile onto a rough lane. Go right, dropping down past the house at Newlands, with its 1746 datestone and mullioned windows, to emerge onto the A635 Greenfield Road.

Go straight across down Black Sike Lane into wooded Hart Holes Clough, and steeply up the other side to a junction, where turn right. *A stone hut bears an Austonley Local Board Waterworks 1889 tablet.* Immediately beyond, as the road opens out at Hogley Green, turn left along a driveway, and keep left at a fork to pass between houses and along to the old hamlet of Hogley. Swing right between the buildings to a gate/stile out into a field. Head away with the wall, crossing to the left side at the corner stile and resuming. From the next stile drop across the field centre to one opposite, then advance with a wall down to a stile onto Cold Well Lane, at a nice corner where a stone slab bridges a streamlet.

Go right just as far as a lone house. *Once a Sunday School of 1816, the key to its origin is etched above the door.* An enclosed grassy path turns down its far side, swinging down to a kissing-gate before a sharp bend at a path junction. Ignore the corner stile and turn left down this broad enclosed way, dropping gently to a gate/stile at the head of wooded Stubbin Clough. The path runs a splendid grassy route above the edge of the clough, and down to join a drive. Down to the left is a pair of millponds. Don't follow the drive down through the houses, but cross straight over, quickly turning left through a gap between houses at Upper Stubbin. Through a gate into a field, a largely stone surfaced path descends to a gate at the bottom, from where Stubbin Lane runs straight down to the A6024 at Hinchliffe Mill. *A mill with its chimney sits beneath the dams, while just along to the left are a shop and the Stumble Inn. Holmfirth Vineyard is just a half-mile distant.*

Cross straight over and bear left on Old Road to an angled crossroads with Ford Gate. *A fine assortment of old houses is passed, including a squat single-storey terrace and contrastingly tall three-storeyed weavers' dwellings.* At the end go straight ahead on Water Street past old millworkers' cottages. Into the mill yard keep straight past the end of the mill itself, to a footbridge on the River Holme. Don't cross, but head downstream on a path between the mill-race and the river. This runs on through wooded surrounds as the watercourse quickly opens out into a large millpond backed by Bottoms Mill at Burnlee. *For a short finish avoiding any further hills, simply remain on the riverside path to ultimately join the A6024 which leads back into Holmfirth.*

Before the end of the pond, drop down to cross a bridge on the adjacent river. Double back a few yards upstream, then take the left fork slanting pleasantly up the pasture to a path crossroads in the centre. Turn left up the path to a stile into Malkin House Wood. A good path slants left through trees, through a cutting beneath an old quarry site. Crossing a level path, the slanting path continues to a gap-stile at the wood top just above, this upper section being dense with hollies. The path continues across two fields to Malkin House. *This proves to be a splendid three-storeyed weaver's house in a lovely setting.* Pass straight on up the drive, through this old hamlet and onto a back road, Brow Lane.

Just a few strides left take a stile on the right and head up the wallside. The path slants left from the corner above, up to another corner stile, then more clearly left to a stile above a stone hut. This accesses the old walled way of Dunsley Bank Road. *Summer Wine devotees might expect to see Compo-like characters ambling along here. Another shorter return turns left down this.* Cross straight over on a short green way to a gap by a gate, through which the splendid walled way of Cartworth Lane crosses a gentle brow and runs unfailingly between fields to the farming hamlet of Cartworth Fold. Joining Cartworth Bank Road, go briefly left to a junction. Below you is the valley of the short-lived River Ribble.

On the very junction a path drops down a few steps to a stile into the top of an unkempt, sloping pasture. A path descends the side, and just beneath a pond a wall-stile puts you on the other side. Descend with the wall, but as it turns off go steeply down to a stile at the field bottom, from where steps drop down to the old Dover Mill site. Go left on the access road past several houses, and after bridging the stream the public footpath rises briefly up the lane, going left on an enclosed path between gardens to drop back onto the access road downstream. This leads past further houses to emerge onto the B6106 Dunford Road on the edge of Holmfirth. *You can go left on the footway to re-enter Holmfirth.* Ideally, cross and ascend the slanting Well Hill Road to quickly reach a crossroads. Go left on Underbank Old Road, passing a variety of interesting dwellings and even having a slight rise with central setts before dropping back down into the centre as South Lane.

MARSDEN CLOUGH

A memorable blend of moorland, reservoirs and cloughs

START *Digley (SE 110072; HD9 2QD)*

DISTANCE *7 miles (11¹⁄₄km)*

ORDNANCE SURVEY 1:25,000 MAP
Explorer OL1 - Peak District, Dark Peak **or**
Explorer 288 - Bradford & Huddersfield

ACCESS *Start from Yorkshire Water car park at north side of Digley Reservoir, under a mile off A6024 at Holmbridge. Holmbridge has bus from Huddersfield.*

Digley Reservoir is a relatively modern addition to the water catchment of the Holme Valley, having arrived on the scene in 1952. The car park has been created in a landscaped quarry which provided stone for construction of the dam. Leave the car park by a gateway on the reservoir side of the entrance, and across a broad path another gap sends a well-used path down a heathery bank above the reservoir to rejoin the road lower down. *At once there are big views over the water to the moorland slopes of Black Hill.*

Continue the short way to a junction at the end of the dam. Don't cross, but continue down the road, soon reaching a kissing-gate on the right. A path runs briefly parallel with the road before slanting down through a small wood, and from a corner kissing-gate descends steps onto Digley Road. Turn left on this for a traffic-free descent into Holmbridge above Digley Brook, the surface improving as the church tower appears in front, emerging past some modern housing and a cricket field. *The village of Holmbridge is based around the confluence of Marsden Clough with the River Holme. Centrepiece is St David's church, with the Bridge pub well placed.*

Turn right over the bridge and go left on a side road signed to Ramsden Reservoir and Yateholme. When it splits take the right branch, Bank Lane. *Set into the wall on the left is a well dated 1834.* The road becomes Brownhill Lane as it climbs to a junction. Keep straight on past several houses to reach the dam of Brownhill Reservoir (1932), continuing on to approach a lay-by just short of Ramsden Reservoir (1892). *The section above Brownhill Reservoir is a charming stroll with increasing views over its colourful banks to the Black Hill skyline. Approaching the Ramsden dam, Holme appears on the hill across, while there is also a grand view up the length of this upper reservoir.*

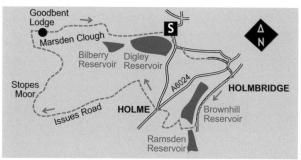

Just short of the dam (and car park beyond) an enclosed track turns down towards the grassy dam, and an enclosed path crosses it just below its crest. *Downstream is the head of Brownhill Reservoir.* At the end the path slants away from the dam, ignoring an early branch left. The good path rises through trees onto a knoll on the spur between the two arms of Brownhill Reservoir. It then runs delightfully above the bank of Netherley Wood until dropping down to a footbridge on Rake Dike, just above a lovely waterfall.

Slanting back up the other side the path levels out to leave the trees at a stile, then up a small rough pasture to adjacent stiles at the top corner above a wood. An enclosed path rises to two small gates: from the left-hand one continue up a fieldside to a gate. *On the left is an architect's self-designed house almost entirely below ground level.* The broader enclosed way runs out onto the A6024 on the edge of Holme: turn left as far as a cobbled square. *En route you pass Holme Castle, a house with a castellated block dating from the 1820s; and opposite it a former school, complete with bell and inscription of 1838: the date 1694 is carved on the door lintel. Holme is a small but historic settlement nestled at the head of the Holme Valley, just within the Peak District National Park's northern boundary. Its attractive cottages include three-storeyed weavers' houses. The Fleece Inn (with shop) and WCs are just along the road, claiming a steady passing trade on the Woodhead Road climbing to Holme Moss.*

Turn right up through the square and along cul-de-sac Meal Hill Road. *Note a 1696 datestone on the arch at the small playground entrance.* The road rises past the former Holme Liberal Club and the school of 1880 to lose its surface as it winds away. At a fork keep left, rising to a patch of open ground graced with a seat. *This enjoys a view of Digley Reservoir, with the Wessenden Head Moor skyline up ahead.* Keep left on the main track, which as Issues Road commences a long, very gradual rise onto Stopes Moor, with some good grass verges at times. Ignore a lesser branch left just before a gate/stile. Ahead are the attractive brows of Issue Edge and Black Dike Head beneath the peaty plateau of Black Hill. On finally shrugging off the walls at a gate the track advances more happily onto the moor, within a quarter-mile reaching a branch right, the walk's summit at 1312ft/400m. This is your grassy path, while ahead is Issue Clough with its rock-walled waterfall.

Bearing right, the branch path curves down with the scant remains of a wall, crossing the headwaters of Hey Clough (and the old wall) and heading away on a good firm footing. *Heather abounds on this section, with Hey Clough deepening down to the right, and Digley Reservoir returning.* It runs a level course along the heathery moor of Good Bent before curving left down to steep-walled Marsden Clough. *Across, the shooting lodge of Goodbent Lodge stands amid a sorry scene of crumbling field walls, while downstream the clough enters a ravine-like enclave.* The track slants down to cross a footbridge at a confluence. *Once known as Blackpool Bridge, it appears superfluous given the decent ford alongside, but is nevertheless a good spot to linger at the delightful merging of Dean Clough and Reap Hill Clough.*

Now leaving the moor, the continuation up the opposite bank is a brief stony pull before swinging back left to rises as a gentler grassy way to a gate. Continue up the old wallside to a stile/gate onto Nether Lane, a roughly-walled track. Turn right down this, past Goodbent Lodge and the old farm of Bartin, becoming fully enclosed as Nether Lane. *Black Hill spreads its shoulders to the right, with Digley Reservoir at times ahead.* The track runs on to a major junction just beyond the barns of Greaves Head. Take the branch down to the right, a similarly wide walled track which drops left as Hoowood Lane above Bilberry Dam to another such junction at a seat on a patch of open ground.

Bilberry Reservoir is a charming spot, looking across it to the steep-walled and immensely colourful Marsden and Hey Cloughs. Its engaging character belies its gruesome past, for this calm oasis was the scene of a major disaster in 1852. Following a cloudburst on the moors, its unstable 12-year old dam burst and a swollen torrent raced down the valley to Holmfirth, taking 81 lives with it along with mills, houses and bridges. Keeping left this runs on before becoming a footpath fringing the trees enclosing Digley Reservoir. Very quickly it rejoins a track at the point where the old sunken way runs forlornly into the engulfing waters. This rises past an old quarry and on to the car park.

Brownhill Reservoir

MELTHAM MOOR

*A bracing tramp in the northern extremities of Peakland,
interspersed with some colourful side valleys*

START *Meltham (SE 099106; HD9 4AE)*

DISTANCE *7¹4 miles (11¹2km)*

ORDNANCE SURVEY 1:25,000 MAP
Explorer OL1 - Peak District, Dark Peak
Explorer 288 - Bradford & Huddersfield

ACCESS *Start from the centre. Car park up Clarke Lane behind
Waggon & Horses (or bigger one up Carlile Street by Post office).
Bus from Huddersfield. • OPEN ACCESS (tiny section), see page 8.*

Meltham is an unassuming but strongly independent cross
between a large village and a small town. Streets featuring shops,
pubs and cafes radiate from near St Bartholomew's church. A 3¹2-
mile branch line from the Huddersfield-Sheffield line at Lockwood
opened in 1868 and fully closed in 1965. Meltham was famed for
production of David Brown tractors, its factory closing in 1988. From
the central junction, with a tiny old school of 1823 on your right,
cross the main road and head along Greens End Road left of the
church. Curving round behind it, go left up suburban Colders Lane.
At the top it narrows at some older houses, and transforms into a
narrow footpath. Rising between walls it emerges onto a road,
Leygards Lane, with the edge of Meltham Moor straight ahead.

Go left to a crossroads with Wessenden Head Road, and straight over onto a broad farm drive, Bedlam Road. *Fine views back over the town feature Meltham Cop, Castle Hill and Emley Moor TV mast.* The track rises away to suddenly emerge on the edge of Royd Edge Clough. *This is a splendid moment: at your feet is the colourful, sweeping valley, its heather-clad flanks rising to a broad skyline of Meltham Moor.* Turn right on the continuing track, rising largely enclosed above the clough edge. At a gate at the top leave the track going left down to Sun Royd Farm, and from a stile to its right, continue up with the wall. A spell in grassy pasture returns you to heather moorland at a kissing-gate. A footpath remains with the wall as a level section leads to another kissing-gate and a resumption of the climb. Rising past a solitary house you reach a stile back onto Wessenden Head Road on the open moor.

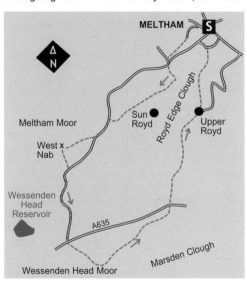

With the rocks of West Nab just above, head up the road for five minutes to a path branching right just after the distinctive Cock Crowing Stone set back to the right. The path crosses a fence-stile to rise pleasantly up the moor, slanting up to gain the edge as the boulders to your right abate. The path runs left the short way past the remains of a stone hut to soon gain the Ordnance Survey column on West Nab amid a cluster of large boulders. *At 1640ft/500m this high point of Meltham Moor is also the highest point reached in this collection of walks.*

Arrival here offers an outstanding panorama in all directions. From this position on the edge of one National Park you can see into the next up the Pennines, with Penyghent and Great Whernside notable landmarks in the Yorkshire Dales. Rolling moorlands include Black Hill to the south and a long sweep of the Saddleworth, Marsden and Calderdale moors to north and west. Man's efforts at piercing the skyline include transmitter masts on Emley Moor and Holme Moss and assorted windfarms, while the sturdy monument on Stoodley Pike adds a more endearing element. Buckstones, Blackstone Edge and Pendle Hill also restore sanity.

Leave by heading south in the direction of the Holme Moss mast. Within yards, on the edge of the rocks, you reach a distinct groove overlooked by a solitary boulder. A thin but clear grassy path drops to its left, angling down the briefly steep slope. Passing a boulder on a stone base, the thin path runs the short way to a fence-stile amid moister ground, just beyond which you are back on Wessenden Head Road. Turn right, passing a Meltham/Marsden boundary stone and tracing a quiet course across the moors with Wessenden down to the right. *Below is Wessenden Head Reservoir, completed in 1881 and the highest of four in the valley that descends to Marsden. Beyond it is Wessenden Head Moor and ahead is Black Hill, while West Nab casts a shapely profile looking back.* Absorbing the reservoir access road, a roadside path runs the short way to the A635 at Wessenden Head. *The Isle of Skye pub welcomed travellers to this isolated spot until demolition in the 1950s.*

Almost on the junction, a ladder-stile to the left puts you onto Wessenden Head Moor. Slanting left the improving path descends by a fence. *Straight ahead, the Pennine Way can be seen coming down off Black Hill.* At a crumbling wall corner the path turns left and remains a splendid route, becoming partly enclosed to run through bracken above a scattered wood. After crossing the head of colourful Snape Clough it becomes enclosed to run the short way to a ladder-stile onto the hairpin bend of a broad track, Springs Road. *Just down to the right is Goodbent Lodge, a shooting lodge, past which are Marsden Clough, Digley Reservoir (joined by Bilberry Reservoir in front) and the upper Holme Valley.* Turn left on the track, a fair portion of which features a two-lane stone causey. *The well-defined grooves were formed by the wheels of horse-drawn carts laden with stone from quarries close by the path.*

At the end the old way rises to a gate back onto the A635. Go right for less than a hundred yards to a gate opposite, from where the bridleway of Magdalen Road heads off up the wallside. Back on moorland, it soon attains a brow revealing Royd Edge Clough again. *West Nab up to the left is part of a splendid picture of the walk's first stage.* The grassy cart track quickly narrows to a broad path, enjoying a grand descent of the moor-side. Through a gate at the bottom corner it becomes enclosed by walls, soon merging into Ash Royd Farm drive. Continue down to a cluster of houses immediately after the first house (Upper Royd) on the left. From a gate on the left before this grouping drop down a small paddock to a gate, from where an initially stony path descends a wallside. Through a gate at the bottom drop to a stile just below, and a grassy path resumes this direct line down through the Woodland Trust's Royd Wood.

Through a kissing-gate at the bottom, drop to a ladder-stile just below, joining a broad path along tree-lined Royd Edge Clough. Go right just a few paces then double back left down a rough path, quickly dropping more directly to meet the better wallside path of Hebble Lane just below. Cross the footbridge just ahead to a broader path, and turn right on this over a former mill-cut. The path rises with a wall above a millpond through to a kissing-gate in front of a bungalow. Go left up the setted access road, soon levelling out and running a short surfaced course to meet another road at Laithe Farm. Descend a few feet to a kissing-gate on the left, and a firm path runs alongside allotments to emerge onto a suburban road. Cross straight over to resume on a short-lived, surfaced course out onto the next street, Tinker Lane. Turn right to emerge onto the main road, and go left the couple of minutes back to the centre. *Passed on your right is the large Odd Fellows Hall of 1851.*

Boundary stone,
Wessenden Head Moor

COLNE VALLEY

A magical mix of moorland, towpath and colourful cloughs

START *Slaithwaite (SE 079139; HD7 5AS)*

DISTANCE *7¹4 miles (11¹2km)*

ORDNANCE SURVEY 1:25,000 MAP
Explorer OL21 - South Pennines

ACCESS *Start from the centre. Old Bank car park. Bus from Huddersfield, Holmfirth, Oldham; Huddersfield-Manchester train.*

Slaithwaite is a typical small Pennine mill-town, which grew from the establishment of large mills in the boom years of the woollen industry. Earlier mills took advantage of the fast-flowing River Colne and its many sidestreams, while the arrival of the Huddersfield Narrow Canal in 1798 was a further boost to the local economy. One of the final pieces of its restoration jigsaw slotted into place in 2001 when the waterway which had disappeared in a culvert across the town centre was fully reinstated. The Free School of 1721 is close by the start at Old Bank. Slaithwaite can also claim to have been a spa town, after a 19th century hydropathic centre was created upon discovery of a mineral spring.

From the mini-roundabout at Britannia Road and Station Road, with your back to the canal turn left along Market Place, passing the Shoulder of Mutton pub and beneath the church of St James. Quickly bear left on Nabbs Lane. *The Silent Woman pub on the right bears evidence of its former name the Globe Inn, and its equally defunct brewer, Bentley & Shaw of Lockwood, just three or four miles away on the edge of Huddersfield. Opposite it on the left is the Manor House, now apartments. A low building alongside is the former lock-up.* The road bears right as Holme Lane, rising beneath a tall railway viaduct. A steep climb leads to a path going right across the dam of Slaithwaite Reservoir. *Locally known as Hill Top Reservoir, it was constructed to supply the canal. Derelict Bank Gate Mill stands to the right.*

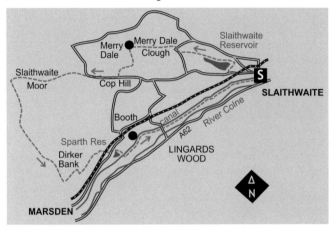

Immediately over the colourful outflow footbridge turn left on a path along the reservoir bank, with a mill-cut on the right. This leads increasingly pleasantly into the wooded environs of the reservoir head. Passing a weir at the start of the mill-cut, the lovely surroundings lead up to the foot of a smaller dam. *This served the departed Clough House Mills, now a wooded area to your right. The right of way continues up the broad track onto a road, then left the short way to Clough House Bridge.* Local preference uses the path over the smaller dam, then right a short way to cross the outflow above a fine waterfall tumbling into a small ravine. The path then goes left to bridge the main stream for a short climb onto a path along the wood top. The path runs right above the edge of the wooded clough and quickly out via a kissing-gate onto a road.

Go right the short way down to Clough House Bridge, over which take a gate on the left and resume upstream into Merry Dale Clough, with the tiny stream for company. Ignoring an early footbridge this is a splendid ramble, a faint path staying close to the tiny stream as it burbles through colourful scrubby pastures. This remains so for some time until reaching an impasse as a grassy bridge crosses the stream. Don't cross but take the path on the right, rising through a tiny cutting and past a lovely pond on the left. A snicket and steps rise past the house at Merry Dale, up with a streamlet to join the drive for the final yards onto setted Tyas Lane, an old packhorse route.

Double back left down this narrow way to a stone-arched bridge in wooded Bradshaw Clough. It winds steeply up the other side as the narrow, variously surfaced bridleway of Scout Lane, through heather and bilberry banks to emerge onto a drive. *A simple option goes straight ahead to a crossroads, then turning right on the road to rejoin the route.* From a small gate on your right at this bend, cross a field centre to a small gate at the end. Not as per map, pass through and rise up the wall's near side to a stile at the top corner. Bear right across this paddock to a fence-stile at a wall corner, and head away along the right-hand field edge. Through a stile/gate at the end you join a driveway, which is followed up and around to a bend to join a road, Cop Hill Side, alongside Wham Farm. *This broad ridge has big open views, left over Marsden's moorland environs of Pule Hill and Marsden Moor, with Slaithwaite Moor just ahead.*

When the road turns right at a junction, go straight ahead along a short-lived walled grassy way to a tiny gate onto a corner of Slaithwaite Moor. The grassy way continues along the wallside to another tiny fence-gate at a wall corner onto the moor proper. The splendid path heads directly away, rising very gently through heather, and ignoring an early lesser left branch. The path rises past a ruined stone hut, and with a ditch alongside grouse butts, rises very gently through heather to a junction by a memorial seat. *At 1246ft/380m this marks the summit of the walk, and on a clear day it offers the ideal backrest to survey a fine view south over Shooter's Nab, Black Hill, Wessenden, Pule Hill, Standedge and Marsden Moor. The tower on Castle Hill above Huddersfield is seen in front of Emley Moor TV mast.*

Turn left to begin a grand descent, swinging left on leaving the heather to drop to cross Old Clough on duckboards. Entering the National Trust's Shaw Heys, over a brow a section of flagging is met. As the adjacent fence turns off, the path drops left to a gate at a fence junction, and a moister section descends Netherwood Heys utilising much of the adjacent old wall. Improving as more heather is reached, continue down to become enclosed by crumbling walls as Huck Hill Lane. The way improves as it bends left, leaving moorland for rougher pastures. A flagged section alongside a track precedes one last wallside track dropping to a kissing-gate onto a grassy access road with Huck Hill Farm on the right. With Marsden outspread below, turn left on this enclosed way, a grand stride through bilberry-draped Dirker Bank. Its steady descent steepens around an old quarry to double back down onto another access road at another house, now on the edge of Marsden.

Go left on Plains Lane above odd houses, and at a junction where it swings uphill, advance to a fork just ahead in front of two houses. The right branch passes along the house front at Ashton Barn to rickety steps down into an overgrown corner. The path runs left a little and on to a small platform to a stile/gate just ahead. Cross a scrubby bank beneath a wood, and along to a stile into the trees of Green Hill Clough. A good path now runs right above the clough edge, dropping down to emerge in front of the railway. The path drops left a short way and out onto an access road junction at Netherwood Lane by the railway. Turn right under the arch out onto Park Gate Road. Just yards to the left a cart track turns down to Sandhill Cottages, passing Sparth Reservoir on the right. *This was built to help supply the canal, and has long been a popular wild swimming venue.* Joining the Huddersfield Narrow Canal, pass along the front of the houses to cross a footbridge alongside Cellars Clough Mills, and take a short path left down onto the towpath.

For more on the canal see WALK 23. Turn right for Slaithwaite, following the towpath all the way back. *Features include a number of descending locks; the occasional company of the River Colne; a lovely corner with a holding basin at Booth; a vertical 'guillotine' gate at Lock 23, due to bridge widening leaving little space for a conventional lock; and a busy setting alongside Upper Mill, which includes a brewery and a bakery/café.* From Upper Mill the tarmac finish is shared with vehicles, with the start just ahead.

BUCKSTONES

Magnificent moorland walking above Standedge Tunnel

START *Marsden (SE 046118; HD7 6DH)*

DISTANCE *7 miles (11¼km)*

ORDNANCE SURVEY 1:25,000 MAP
Explorer OL21 - South Pennines

ACCESS *Start from the railway station, adjacent car park. Train from Huddersfield and Manchester, bus from Huddersfield and Oldham. • OPEN ACCESS: National Trust land, see page 8.*

For a note on Marsden see WALK 24. Facing the station, go left to join the Huddersfield Narrow Canal at a lock, and go left on the towpath for a pleasant ten minutes. Passing under low railway bridges you emerge opposite a visitor centre in a restored warehouse at Tunnel End: just past it, rise to a bridge. *The canal's focal point also features a café by Standedge Tunnel entrance. Boat trips range from short forays into the tunnel to full-length journeys. Alongside, the railway enters its own tunnel. The canal was built to convey goods between towns on either side of the Pennines, a 20-mile route linking with canals at Huddersfield and Dukinfield. 42 locks raised it 436ft to Marsden, with 32 locks on the west to Diggle. The impasse of Standedge called for the highest, deepest and (at more than 3 miles) longest canal tunnel in the land. Until its opening in 1811, goods had to be unloaded and carried over Standedge, a route the canal horses still took after completion while the boatmen 'legged' their way through the tunnel by working their feet along its walls.*

Railway competition soon hit hard, though it wasn't until 1944 that the tunnel finally closed. Fast forward 30 years, and with just six locks remaining open, enthusiasts embarked upon a restoration programme that culminated at the start of the 21st century in the re-opening of Standedge Tunnel. The railway runs a parallel course under Standedge, with two tunnels completed in 1848 and 1871: advantage of the canal was taken to remove the spoil by boat. Increasing demand brought about the construction of a third tunnel in 1894, and this is now the only one in use.

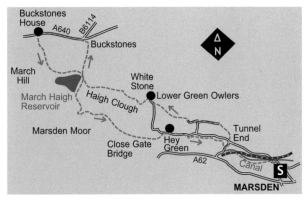

Cross the bridge and head up the road to a junction with Waters Road in front of the former Tunnel End Inn (closed in 2012). Climb past it, through a gate and up a path alongside a driveway. Pass left of the house above, up the tapering garden to a gate onto a rough access road: turn left past several dwellings. *Grand views look ahead over the uppermost Colne Valley backed by a big moorland sweep.* Becoming surfaced, you soon reach a junction: don't drop away, but take the right option maintaining a higher course to two more houses. It ends abruptly just before the last one where a walled footway takes over, passing to its right. Quickly emerging into open slopes beneath Great Edge it advances invitingly away, rising gently to reach a bridle-gate in a fence. *This affords a first view ahead to the March Hill and Buckstones skyline.*

The path drops slightly, winding round to the right and on past a low ruin. *Pule Hill's craggy edge impresses to the south.* A flagged path drops to a streamlet in Park Clough, across which double back a few yards then climb a wallside to a gate at the top. Joining a narrow road turn right past white-walled Lower Green Owlers and down to a dip at Green Owlers Clough. Go left on the rough road above the clough to the moor edge. At a fork take the more inviting track left, remaining enclosed to rise to White Hall. Here take a stile by a gate on the left onto the grassy moor, and a broad path heads invitingly away. *Haigh Clough appears ahead, with March Haigh Reservoir's embankment beneath the knoll of March Hill.*

Soon approaching a sidestream, ignore an obvious right branch slanting up to a nearby fence corner, and keep straight on to cross the streamlet on four stone slabs. The path now enjoys a splendid march along the rim of Haigh Clough, with gentler rising moorland on your right. This near-level course is maintained until arrival at a flat, stone-arched bridge on a sidestream. *Note a nice waterfall downstream.* Without crossing, bear right on a thinner path ascending its near side, soon going left to bridge it, and along the short way to the outflow of March Haigh Reservoir. *This was built by the canal company in the mid 1800s.*

Turn right on a path running 30 yards to a fork: you shall return to this point. Take the less obvious right branch, rising gently to the channeled stream you recently crossed. Across, resume the gentle rise, with the Buckstones high above. The next ten minutes is the walk's only rough section, crossing tussocky, part moist terrain. The unkempt path forges gently on up to a kissing-gate in a fence, and a transformed path rises away, within 30 yards reaching a fork. The less obvious right-hand option commences a splendid, steeper climb towards the Buckstones: breaking through the bouldery escarpment you gain the walk's high point at 1480ft/451m. Hidden from view just 50 yards above is a car park on the A640.

The Buckstones form a typical gritstone 'edge'. At the car park a National Trust board introduces Buckstones to motorists, who can effortlessly survey the greater part of the trust's 5685-acre Marsden Moor estate. Directly below is March Haigh Reservoir, while beyond Pule Hill are Black Hill and Holme Moss mast. Without rising to the car park, take a path left on the crest, fading as the rocks do, and slanting a few yards up onto the road. Go left, the rocks ending but re-forming on the right as you trace the road to isolated Buckstones House. *Until around 2000 this was the Buckstones Inn.*

A kissing-gate opposite sends a path down the moorland slope, soon entering bracken. The grassy path emerges to continue down the slightly moist moor before swinging left to cross duckboards to meet another path at a catchwater drain. Go left, soon emerging from bracken to run a good course with the drain, with the reservoir to your right. At an old sluice gate just short of the dam, the path drops right to the earlier junction above the outflow. Retrace steps to the outflow, crossing it to head off along the reservoir's grassy embankment path. At the far end, the path rises a few feet then heads away alongside a redundant catchwater, its level course quickly running to meet a firm, broader path at a stone post. *This is the Rapes Highway, a splendid packhorse route over which trains of ponies would have regularly toiled during the 17th and 18th centuries carrying goods between Marsden and Milnrow. The marker post inscribed 'PH Road' is one of half a dozen erected in 1908.*

Turn left down this for an infallible gentle descent of the moor. Passing another stone post, the path soon becomes stone-flagged until just short of the head of Willykay Clough. Across this the path runs on, featuring further flags to drop into Stonepit Lee Clough. A stonier descent above this deeper clough drops down to a confluence. Bear right for a minute on a broader path to arrive at Close Gate Bridge. *This graceful packhorse bridge overlooks another confluence in a delightful setting: it is better known as Eastergate Bridge, a corruption of Esther's Gate, named after the landlady of the Packhorse Inn that stood nearby.*

Leave the moor by crossing the bridge, and a good path runs downstream the short way to a bridle-gate onto Blake Lea Lane opposite Eastergate Cottage. Turn right on the road, dropping a little to level out at Hey Green House to pass a generator. *Dating from around 1890, it used water-power to provide electricity to light mill-owner Joseph Crowther's 'big house'.* After the terrace of Lower Hey Green, take a bridle-gate on the right. A firm path runs alongside the beck, a splendid stride alongside the drained Tunnel End Reservoir. At the end drop right between an attractive terrace and the grassy embankment to a gateway onto a road. Cross straight over and down a grassy area to return to Tunnel End. All that remains is to retrace opening steps along the towpath.

WESSENDEN

Exploring the Peak District's northernmost valley

START *Marsden (SE 047116; HD7 6DJ)*

DISTANCE *7¼ miles (11½km)*

ORDNANCE SURVEY 1:25,000 MAP
Explorer OL1 - Peak District, Dark Peak
Explorer OL21 - South Pennines

ACCESS *Start from Towngate, outside church. Roadside parking.*
Bus from Huddersfield and Oldham, train from Huddersfield and
Manchester. • OPEN ACCESS: see page 8 (section avoidable).

Sheltering in a great bowl of the Pennines beneath Pule Hill, Marsden is the first settlement in the Colne Valley. Large textile mills and terraced rows typify this once manufacturing dominated village - the Colne Valley was a hotbed of unrest when the Luddite movement was in full ferment. Outside St Bartholomew's church is the tomb of machine-maker Enoch Taylor: those who feared the machines would take their jobs famously gave his name to the tools they used to smash them. The large church sits a reasonable distance from the modest little shopping streets: alongside is shapely Mellor Bridge of 1772. Despite being in the Colne Valley, Marsden is home to Holme Valley Mountain Rescue Team, and has its own brewery. The Huddersfield Narrow Canal passes through just short of Standedge Tunnel, of which more in WALK 23.

From the church cross Towngate to a little green with stocks and Enoch Taylor's grave. Go straight ahead to a bridge and into the Market Place. Advance to the front of the Mechanics Hall, then turn right past the shops up Peel Street. Cross the A62 at the top and continue up alongside a park. At a T-junction with Carrs Road, go left a few yards then take a drive doubling back uphill. A stiff pull leads to its demise at the very top, entering the yard of a house in front. Go left between stables and house to a gate in front of another house. Here turn sharp right between garden fences to a short flight of stone steps sending a path up into open country. The path rises as a sunken way towards moorland slopes, quickly slanting right. *Squeezing between bilberry bushes, grand views look back over the town, with Pule Hill and Buckstones high above.*

The old way soon levels out, running a splendid, largely enclosed way beneath Binn Edge's colourful slopes. *Ahead is sprawling moorland, and down to your right is Bank Bottom Mills beneath Pule Hill.* Advance through a small gate, and after a kissing-gate it runs behind the ruinous buildings of Binn House, then

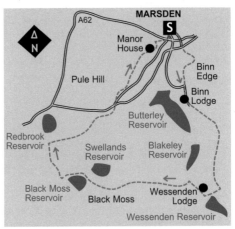

rises slightly to a gate into Peters Farm. Continue along the short drive running out onto a hairpin bend of Binn Lane. Go left, briefly uphill then along for a short half-mile, serving several houses before losing its surface after Binn Lodge Farm. *Briefly glimpsed below during this section is Butterley Reservoir, completed in 1906 as the last of the valley's four reservoirs, and by far the largest.*

Just a few yards further the track also ends. *You are greeted by a magnificent prospect of Wessenden, with Blakeley Reservoir cradled in a moorland bowl.* Pass through a bridle-gate in front onto the National Trust's Binn Moor, and two paths head away. The right one slants down through open country to a substantial stone-arched bridge in Rams Clough. Rise up the other side alongside a wall, soon easing at a low ruin on your left. *Just past here a gate on the right sends a path off across unkempt pastures, a useful, waymarked alternative for dog-walkers.* Continue up, with a reedy hollow between you and the wall. A little further, the path slants more determinedly left to quickly rise to a fine stone-arched bridge on the redundant reedy catchwater drain of Deer Hill Conduit.

Turn right on the embanked grassy path to commence a lengthy, level stride in its company. Several old bridges are passed, and a stile crossed at the head of Great Clough. *Excellent views look over both Blakeley and Butterley reservoirs backed by moorland.* After another stile the drain abruptly ends, but the path maintains its course across the moorland of Hey Brinks, entering bracken. *Ahead appears Black Hill and the Holme Moss mast beyond the bracken-draped valley head.* Very shortly Wessenden Reservoir is revealed below, and only yards further a path branches right, virtually in line with the dam, descending steeply through dense bracken. At the bottom it runs a few level strides right onto a wallside path, doubling back left the few yards further to meet the Pennine Way path alongside the dam. *This, the valley's oldest reservoir, was built as long ago as 1790 to operate waterwheels in the Colne Valley, and enlarged 50 years later.*

Turn down a few yards to pass a bridge over the outflow and continue down the ensuing rough road past Wessenden Lodge. *This former Edwardian shooting lodge has also been a farm serving the Yorkshire classic 'ham & egg teas': refreshments were still available when Wainwright researched his Pennine Way guide in the late 1960s. For a much shorter return, remain on this all the way back.* After a short while leave by a steep path doubling back down to a footbridge on Wessenden Brook, a lovely spot. A steep ascent up the other side meets a contouring path alongside a water company installation. *This offers a good view down over Blakeley Reservoir, while looking back, Raven Rocks on Meltham Moor top the skyline above Wessenden Lodge.* Turn right on this splendid level path along to cross Blakely Clough. Steps then take it up onto the open moor, rising pleasantly with the diminishing clough. A short flagged section is precursor to a long flagged spell.

On levelling out, the clough ends on the watershed, and the flags maintain an easy march to Black Moss Reservoir. *Just beneath it is Swellands Reservoir, with Pule Hill beyond. Both reservoirs, along with soon to be seen Redbrook, were built to supply the Huddersfield Narrow Canal.* A path crosses a low embankment to a sandy beach at the other corner. Intermittent flags briefly return as the path runs on to a fence before swinging left to a gateway at a fence junction. Flags now feature for a considerable time as you reach a junction with a path from the main embankment.

Turning right the flags rise to a kissing-gate in the fence on a modest brow on Rocher Moss: Redbrook Reservoir appears below. The path descends to meet a broad, contouring path at a breached embankment. *This was the second turnpike road over Standedge, completed in 1815 by the celebrated John Metcalfe (Blind Jack of Knaresborough). A standing stone is inscribed 'M11 720 yards'.* While the PW goes left, take the pitched path on the other side of the gap and turn right, over a streamlet and gently rising past a pool to a brow on Warcock Hill. *Pule Hill now dominates the scene.* The track begins a long, steady descent of the moor, ignoring branches to the left, to join Mount Road after crossing the scarred hollow of Carr Clough. *Mount Road is part of the first turnpike route across Standedge, which continued west via Thieves Clough (see WALK 25). The present A62 to the north of Pule Hill traces the third turnpike of 1839.*

Cross straight over and along Old Mount Road. *This was the earlier turnpike route out of Marsden created by Blind Jack in 1759.* Almost at once bear left on Hades Farm drive. This runs for some time along the moor edge before dropping gently down. *Below, Bank Bottom Mills feature again, with Butterley Reservoir at the entrance to Wessenden.* Keep on until the drive swings left, just after the second of two paths branching down to the right. Here, as the wall returns, advance the short way down the wallside to a corner gate off the moor. A sunken way winds down between crumbling walls, soon revealing Manor House Farm below. Through a gate go left of the fine old building, down the yard to a gate into a field at the bottom. Descend alongside a deep-set hollow way, winding down to a stile in the corner. Just below, a house drive leads down to the right to Old Mount Road. Go left to the Towngate junction with the main road.

MARSDEN MOOR

Packhorse and turnpike trails meet the Pennine Way

START Standedge (SE 018094; OL3 5LT)

DISTANCE 7$\frac{1}{4}$ miles (11$\frac{1}{2}$km)

ORDNANCE SURVEY 1:25,000 MAP
Explorer OL1 - Peak District, Dark Peak
Explorer OL21 - South Pennines

ACCESS Start from Brun Clough Reservoir car park on A62 summit at Standedge. Huddersfield-Oldham bus. • OPEN ACCESS: see page 8.

Although for convenience the walk starts in Lancashire, be assured it is largely in West Yorkshire. The crest of Standedge sits on the Pennine watershed, and Brun Clough Reservoir was one of many built to supply the Huddersfield Narrow Canal: canal and rail tunnels run directly beneath. Cross the road and follow the Pennine Way north along a rising track. At an early T-junction bear left, and shortly after absorbing the Pennine Bridleway, the PW is signed off right at a kissing-gate. An inviting path ascends moor-grass slopes, and just before a first kissing-gate in a fence, leave on a fainter path curving right. This crosses rough tracks on a short, level walk to a fence-stile onto the National Trust's Close Moss. Ahead rises Pule Hill, with Shooter's Nab and West Nab on the more distant skyline right. You are on the route of a turnpike road built in 1759 by the celebrated John Metcalfe (Blind Jack of Knaresborough).

Advance straight along an improving grassy path, on a gentle decline becoming stone-flagged to suddenly arrive at Thieves Clough Bridge. *This stone-arched structure makes a splendid sight in the midst of sombre moorland, a remarkable survivor from turnpike days. As you descend from the moor here, your route is also on the line of a Roman road.* Resume on the part-flagged path alongside the clough down to another NT sign in front of a fence, air shaft and spoil heaps. *Happily preserved but hidden from here is a tall, imposing stone building, an engine winding-house which helped extract spoil during construction of Standedge Tunnels. Behind is the now dominant crest of Pule Hill above the Carriage House pub on the A62.*

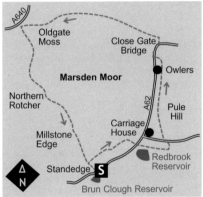

Leave the flagged path and go right over a tiny stream and a grassy path shadows an old catchwater drain around to a kissing-gate onto the A62 at the former Great Western pub. *Named from the railway line beneath it, this closed in 2015.* Cross the road and head along Redbrook Reservoir's grassy dam, also built to supply the canal. Over the outflow footbridge keep straight on a clear path across grassy moor, soon meeting a catchwater at a tiny arched bridge. The path continues on a low embankment alongside it until it turns sharp right, then the path angles left down towards Mount Road. At a cross-path turn left to gain the road summit. *Here you are briefly back on the line of the first turnpike road.* Double back left for 150 yards and turn right on an inviting grassy path along the base of 1433ft/437m Pule Hill. *This is Boat Lane, by which canal ponies were led over Standedge to Diggle while their boats were 'legged' through the three-mile tunnel below.*

The path runs a fine, near-level course beneath Pule Hill's craggy edge to arrive above a red-brick structure. *This and the one above are air-shafts providing ventilation for the tunnels below.*

101

Alongside are the remains of another engine house. Here you cross adjacent grassy ways ascending to the right. Both these served old quarries above, the first being an incline down which stone was carried, and the second an access track. Advance straight on a little more faintly, passing round the base of a big spoil heap beneath the upper shaft, and over a cross-paths with one rising from a lay-by. With the crags above now ended, your thin but clear path advances on, dropping gently through a moist section to a stile in a fence ahead. Just below is the A62. Head across this agreed route on a brief section of non-access land through a rough pasture: briefly pathless, slant slightly down to a stile back into NT land. With the former Coach & Horses pub just below, the improved path heads on above a wall again to a white house at Owlers. Just past a second house, a makeshift gate on the left sends a short, enclosed path down to a stile onto the road.

Cross and follow the footway right. *The building on your left is the former Shepherd's Boy pub, closed in 1920.* At the bend turn down the walled grassy footway of Dark Lane on the left, dropping steeply into Redbrook Clough. Cross the stream and turn right a few yards along the moor foot to Close Gate Bridge. *This graceful packhorse bridge overlooks a confluence in a delightful setting: it is better known as Eastergate Bridge, a corruption of Esther's Gate, named after the landlady of the Packhorse Inn that once stood nearby.* Without crossing the bridge, head away left on the main path by Haigh Clough. *You are now on the Rapes Highway, a splendid packhorse route over which trains of ponies would have regularly toiled during the 17th and 18th centuries carrying goods, principally wool, between Marsden and Milnrow. The route is lined by marker posts inscribed 'PH Road', erected in 1908 by Marsden Town Council: you will pass six of these.*

Within yards the path forks: ignore the right branch dropping to cross the main beck, as yours starts a steep climb out of the foot of Stonepit Lee Clough on your left. Easing out, it bears right across open moor - incorporating a flagged section - to cross the stream at the head of Willykay Clough above a small waterfall. *Difficult to visualise is the scene of devastation here after a major moorland fire in the mid 1990s, as the extensive damage has been eradicated by the efforts of the National Trust and hard-working volunteers who restored much of the vegetation.*

A gentler climb across Close Moss now begins, including a stone-flagged spell. *Ahead is the dome of March Haigh Hill.* This sustained but ever gentle rise across the vast moor again features flagged sections and bilberry patches. On a brow comes a slight drop to cross Willmer Green Clough before rising left with it, again substantially flagged. This infallible course leads steadily up onto Oldgate Moss, rising right of it to a brow revealing the A640 Rochdale-Huddersfield road ahead. Becoming flagged, the path drops slightly to Haigh Gutter beneath a roadside lay-by. On reaching the gate the Pennine Way comes in from the left, so it's straight back onto the moor, across Haigh Gutter to follow this famous route's firm course southwards. Over a gentle brow it drops to a fence corner in a dip. The fence remains company as a short pull precedes a gentle rise over the moor. A similarly gentle drop sees arrival at some boulders in a minor nick at the start of the gritstone edge of Northern Rotcher. *Below are Castleshaw's twin reservoirs.* Turn left/south on the path to begin a splendid stride along the crest of the scarp.

When these rocks abate the path runs on to rise gently to the shorter-lived grouping at Millstone Edge. The route passes the flat-topped Dinner Stone to reach a concrete Ordnance Survey column, at 1470ft/448m the summit of the walk. *Almost at the walk's end this is a stage to savour as the weathered rock formations look*

down on Diggle and southwards to the hills above Saddleworth. Just before it a memorial stone recalls Ammon Wrigley, a local poet and Saddleworth expert. Resuming, the path drops gently to a kissing-gate off the moor proper, and down to an old wall gateway. Kinking slightly left it runs alongside another old wall on your right to the kissing-gate from the walk's early steps. With Brun Clough Reservoir and its car park just below, retrace outward steps to finish.

Northern Rotcher

INDEX · *Walk number refers*